Internal Affairs: How to Mend a Wounded Soul

Richard A. Davis

Published in 2018
Printed in the United States of America

Cover design: Riley Hayes Advertising, Minneapolis, Minnesota, USA

ISBN-10: 0-692-91678-4
ISBN-13: 978-0-692-91678-0

Dedicated to all those I've had the privilege of knowing, serving, and loving down through the years.

Contents

PROLOGUE

After living and working in Europe for 16 years, my wife Susan and I moved back to the USA to be near family and friends in our retirement. The year was 2015, and the 2016 presidential election was just revving up. We quickly discovered that our homeland had changed...and changed radically. We were slammed by a tsunami of media mayhem, political polarization, cultural tribalism, moral confusion, and — worst of all — the hysteria of widespread emotional volatility. We've made several international moves and lived as expats abroad, so culture shock is nothing new to us. But returning to our home country and feeling like strangers in a strange land? This caught us off-guard.

Sadly, things have not settled down in the time since our return. If anything, the dynamics I've listed above have only intensified. The transition of national leadership has been anything but smooth and, as I see it, has brought out the worst in people. Enmity. Hostility. Super-sensitivity. It's as if our country is in perpetual crisis mode — fearful, suspicious, and quick to overreact. It doesn't matter which side of the divide you're on, the emotional temperatures are boiling over. Respectful dialogue is a thing of the past. Objective journalism has succumbed to biased propaganda, and the media are driven by vanity, self-promotion, and ratings. The two forces behind our current culture war are human pride and lust for wealth and power, demons that have tormented our souls and dragged us into chaos ever since we populated the planet.

This book is the result of my attempt to come to terms with these changes in America. What I've discovered is that any disruption in our world is not caused by external factors but by factors within every one of us. External affairs are not robbing us of our peace, balance, and common sense, *internal* affairs are. What's happening around us has merely exposed what's happening within us. We have allowed the things over which we have no control to take control of our thoughts, moods, and emotions. Are we helpless victims? Or are there ways we can regain our composure and liberate our captive hearts?

7

I believe we are not as lost as we "feel" like we are. There is hope. And that's why I've written this book...to help us find our way to higher and firmer ground.

In my previous book, *God, I Don't Get It: Critical Thinking on Critical Questions*, I attempted to answer some of the mega questions people have asked down through the years. How can we know God exists? What is the purpose of the universe, and how do we fit into it? What are the natures of good and evil? Is there a heaven, and is there a hell? If there is eternal life, what can we know about it? Daunting subjects all. In a sense, that book was the first volume, and this is the second. First, we explored the outer universe, and now we will delve into the inner universe. Both journeys are fraught with mystery and are equally challenging, and both involve gathering knowledge and gaining wisdom. But these two enterprises are quite different. Knowledge comes as a result of collecting external information, but wisdom comes in developing an inner sense of learning how to use such information. Knowledge educates, but wisdom liberates.

Each chapter focuses on one of the emotional states in which we find ourselves today, the shifting moods that hit our psyche like breakers on a beach. Just as medical science has yet to conquer the seemingly boundless frontier of the human brain, so it is in our relentless quest to understand the human soul. What complicated, paradoxical creatures we are! Fragile, but resilient. Habitual, but unpredictable. Sensible, but foolish. Prideful, but insecure. As it is in outer space, so it is in inner space: light and darkness coexist in competition.

It is not my intention to offer an answer book or set of strategies guaranteed to dismantle the psychological barriers that may be blocking your way. I distrust any program that suggests health and fulfillment are achieved by completing a few simple steps or applying a formula. While I understand our attraction to easy answers and packaged fixes, there are no detours around the treacherous turns along the road of life. Let's face it, life is complicated. We need to admit it and keep moving.

—

To keep you moving in the right direction, I will share some insights and coping tools I've picked up during my six-plus decades of living and working with people of all kinds. Having spent the better part of my life in ministry, I've been granted unique access to people's private and public spaces, both secular and sacred. And I've ridden the roller coaster of emotion myself, ascending and descending repeatedly and learning three invaluable lessons along the way.

The first lesson is that we should not trust our emotions. God has given us the capacity to feel for many reasons, primarily to experience the fullness of life and thrive, not merely survive. But feelings must never replace truth. While our emotions influence our decisions, they shouldn't dictate them. Even though much of what follows involves the study of our emotions, my goal is to help protect you from being manipulated by yours.

The second lesson is that the primary—if not sole—purpose of life is relationships (both vertical and horizontal). The degree to which we find fulfillment in this world depends on the quality of our relationships, first with God (the vertical) and then with other people (the horizontal). If we fail in either or both of these relational directions, life isn't worth living. From beginning to end, the relationships we establish in this life will determine our satisfaction here…and in the world to come.

The third lesson is that the only thing we have that is real and vital in life is the present moment. Because this is one of my core convictions, I will say more about this later, giving it special attention in the epilogue. How sad it is to squander energy on useless side-trips into the past—which is gone—or into the future—which isn't here yet!

If we get stuck in the past or obsess over the future, we suffer emotional damage and miss out on the wonders of every moment. Even though this should be obvious, we still seem to forget it.

As amazing as life is, there's no doubting it is a battle. As the late psychotherapist and author M. Scott Peck said in the opening sentence of his brilliant book *The Road Less Traveled*, "Life is difficult."

Accepting Peck's premise—and assuming that we all have battle scars—I offer this book as a triage clinic for wounded souls. I hope you find something in these pages to lighten your load, ease your pain, and heal the wounds in your soul.

In faith,
Richard A. Davis

Chapter 1
ABANDONMENT

Why, Lord, do you stand far off? Why do you hide yourself in times of trouble? – **Psalm 10:1**

"They say that abandonment never heals. I say that only an abandoned child never forgets." – **Mario Balotelli**

"I am not so different in my history of abandonment from anyone else after all. We have all been split away from the earth, each other, ourselves." – **Susan Griffin**

And at three in the afternoon Jesus cried out in a loud voice, "Eloi, Eloi, lema sabachthani?" (which means "My God, my God, why have you forsaken me?"). – **Mark 15:34**

    The boy froze in his tracks, seized by panic amidst the swirling colors and shapes of the big city art museum. Where were his parents? Only a moment ago they'd been just ahead of him. How had he allowed them to slip out of sight? Hadn't his father sternly warned him to stay close and not wander? A wave of nausea swept over him as he gasped for breath in the crowd of strangers. Suddenly he took off, running from room to room, desperate to find a familiar face. He bolted out the exit and into the adjacent park. His eyes searched the crowd. People were strolling by, and others were basking in the sun or enjoying a picnic lunch. Tears filled his eyes. He was lost and alone. Abandoned.

    As you were reading the previous paragraph, you may have felt a familiar knot forming in the pit of your stomach. Rooted within our psyche is the gnawing fear that, at times, we will be entirely alone, separated from loved ones and left to fend for ourselves in a hostile, impersonal world. Worse yet, there is the even greater fear that this separation may be permanent.

David: a story of abandonment and guilt

It's apparent to me that Psalm 27:9-10 was written by someone who had experienced the icy grip of abandonment. We believe that that "someone" was King David himself. Here was a man who had known God's paternal love but later felt orphaned by his heavenly Father. Verses 9-10 are his plaintive cry: *"Do not hide your face from me, do not turn your servant away in anger; you have been my helper. Do not reject me or forsake me, God my Savior."* In other words, "Father, don't disappear! Don't expose me to your anger! Don't push me away and leave me on my own! Please, God, PLEASE. Don't do it!"

This is more than a request for God to make His presence known; it's a scream of despair based on a feeling that God has permanently departed. Feeling forsaken. While we rarely use that word anymore, it describes the state of feeling — or even being — utterly alone, condemned to a kind of solitary confinement regardless of how many people may be around us. In this case, we find David feeling the worst kind of abandonment: forsaken by his ultimate Protector.

Even those who profess belief in a caring God are not immune from fear of divine abandonment. Just look at the titles on the shelves of our Christian bookstores. *Where Is God When It Hurts? Disappointment with God. No Man Is An Island. He is There and He is Not Silent. Escape from Loneliness. When Bad Things Happen to Good People. The Pursuit of God.* The popularity of these books bears witness to our dread of being left in the eternal lurch, having to grope in the dark for a God who may not even be there. Either God has moved on to bigger and better things without us, or, worse yet, He doesn't exist and never has.

Consider David's reflections in Psalm 27. They mirror our own emotional and spiritual yearnings. David pleads with the Divine, *"Do not hide your face from me, do not turn your servant away in anger; you have been my helper. Do not reject me or forsake me, God my Savior."*

The underlying emotion here is fear—David's fear that God has turned His back on him. But there's something more. Why would someone who at one time had so much confidence in God now be worried that God had rejected him?

One word explains it: Guilt. While David doesn't openly admit to having feelings of guilt, given what we know about his life, it's hard to believe he wasn't struggling with the sins of his past. Lust. Adultery. Murder. Deception. Covetousness. Pride. Here is a godly man who did some very ungodly things. And when conscientious people do bad things, they're prone to fall into a permanent state of guilt and shame. Because they know deep down that they have turned away from God, they fear He may turn away from them. Our feelings about God usually reveal more about our own disposition than about His.

Abandoned by God: fact or feeling?

There's an anonymous quote bandied about in Christian circles: "If you don't feel close to God, guess who moved?" In one sense, this has the ring of truth. Those who feel far from God can find themselves in a mess of their own making. It's easy to get lost while doing our own thing rather than attending to the things of God. After all, staying in touch with God requires some effort on our part, but ignoring Him takes no effort whatsoever. Laziness and procrastination come naturally to us. That's why spiritual devotion always requires discipline. Our relationship with God is in many ways no different than any other relationship. If we don't make the effort, it won't last. Like the boy in the art museum, all it takes to get lost is to stop paying attention to where we are. And many of us are out there alone, wandering.

Let's consider the "guess who moved" quote more carefully. If I think I am the one responsible for my feelings of separation from the Creator, I may be stuck in a false assumption. Is it possible to feel abandoned by God without having done anything wrong? I believe it is. The key word here is "feel." Feelings aren't facts.

13

Just because I feel far from God doesn't mean I am actually separated from Him. For example, individuals who are depressed — clinically or otherwise — feel abandoned and isolated, but these feelings may have nothing to do with any wrongdoing on their part. In fact, by adding guilt to their feeling of abandonment, their depression deepens. Blame only makes misery worse. We will examine this in more detail in Chapter 3.

Just because we don't sense God's presence doesn't mean He isn't there. The sun is shining even on overcast days; it's just that the clouds keep us from seeing it. God's love for us has nothing to do with how much of His love we feel. That's why we shouldn't mistake feelings for facts. Our feelings come and go, but God's compassion is not so fickle. What would it take to get a parent to abandon his or her child? Our parental instincts are remarkably strong, but God's are even stronger. Is our heavenly Father less committed to His children than we are to ours? Hardly. Our faithfulness is natural, but God's is supernatural.

Having said that, if I do feel something missing in my relationship with God, it's wise to check my conscience for stains and strains. Is there unresolved guilt in my life? Have I walled myself off from Him? If so, my feelings of abandonment may indeed be the result of my wandering. And if that's the case, it's likely that I've wandered away from others as well. We tend to project our whole bundle of relational insecurities onto God and then blame Him for everything. Such is our selfish nature and our resistance to taking responsibility. God is an easy target. However, if after diligent self-examination we can't find anything we've done that would account for our sense of estrangement from God, then what else could it be? Ah, that is the question!

Emma's story

Not all abandonment is the result of intentional human actions or divine causes. Sometimes it's situational. I recently had a long conversation with a young woman — I'll call her Emma — who has long felt a profound sense of being abandoned in life.

14

She couldn't hide the bitterness and disappointment she felt toward God and others. The problem was that when Emma was 25 years old her parents sold their home and moved overseas to live and work. Since Emma chose to remain in the States, for years there had been a physical distance between her and her parents, and they had seen each other only occasionally.

The longer I listened to Emma, the more I realized that she was angry and hurt that her parents had chosen to move away rather than stay in close proximity to her. Even though she didn't say it, it was evident to me that she felt abandoned. Because her folks sold her childhood home, Emma felt that she no longer had a home. Her parents had been her emotional home, and they had run away. Or that's how it felt to Emma. And she took it personally. To make matters worse, Emma knew her feelings weren't rational. She knew her parents were fulfilled in their life abroad, so how could she begrudge them that? After all, wasn't she a grown-up who should be content in her independence? Try as she might, Emma couldn't shake the sensation of homelessness, not having a place where she could go to reconnect with her past and find comfort and support. Even though Emma knew that her parents were alive and well and still attentive and loving toward her, she simply couldn't shake the feeling of having been left on her own.

So what is Emma to do about her overwhelming sense of abandonment? Who can she blame? How can she fix it? Should she ask her parents to give up their life overseas and move back to be close to her? These are perplexing questions, but they show how complicated it is to find healing when we feel as if we are all alone in the world. There are countless reasons why people feel abandoned, but, in many cases, there are neither obvious causes nor simple solutions. This is why it's wise to dig deeper.

The power of an overbearing parent

One of my favorite devotional resources is *Every Day With Jesus*, a quarterly publication by the late British pastor and writer Selwyn Hughes.

One reading is entitled "Problem Fathers?" and in it we find this provocative statement: "Behind most problem children you will find a problem father...statistics will support the assertion that fathers tend to come down more heavily on their children than mothers." I've thought about this long and hard, and it's occurred to me that I have taken on the role of disciplinarian in my own home. My wife Susan is the sympathetic, compassionate one, and I am the enforcer. She's the good cop; I'm the bad.

I have no way of proving it, but my suspicion is that it's like this for many families. The reasons why are debatable, but it seems that men feel obligated to teach their children how to survive in a world of hard knocks, so they push them harder than their mothers do. Most women want their children to grow up feeling secure and loved, so they try to shield their kids from the aches and pains of the cold, cruel world. Dad takes on the role of drill sergeant, and mom becomes the nurse.

I know generalizations about gender roles are not politically correct, but my experience has convinced me that certain things are *generally* true whether we admit it or not. In fact, every culture has its generalizations—call them proverbs, aphorisms, truisms, etc.—which provide a nucleus of wisdom to guide us through life. To deny these nuggets of insight is foolhardy. While there are exceptions to any generalization, God has created us male and female and called us into marital partnership to bring balance to our parenting.

Selwyn Hughes goes on to say, "Coming down hard on children crushes their sensitive spirits...endless criticism, harsh punishments, unrealistic expectations will have their effect in the long run. Many a child who is timid, fearful, and plagued with deep feelings of inferiority and guilt has developed those characteristics not so much by nature as by nurture." I think Mr. Hughes is right. I've found that many who suffer from spiritual insecurity have experienced psychological and/or physical abuse in their past. What starts in the home resurfaces in other relationships. And this seems to be especially true when it comes to our relationship with our earthly father.

David's father(s)

It is not my intention to psychoanalyze David, but I have to wonder what he felt when his biological father, Jesse, sent him away as a young boy to work for the mentally disturbed and abusive master, King Saul. And later, where was Jesse when his son stepped out to face the giant Goliath and an entire army of Philistines hell-bent on killing him? Later still, how did David feel when Saul, who had become like a father to him, launched spears at him and dispatched soldiers to hunt him down and kill him? Where were David's paternal protectors — human and divine — in the midst of these traumatic crises?

As you read Psalm 27:10, keep David's story in mind. *"Though my father and mother forsake me, the Lord will receive me."* Why did David write that? Could it be that he felt abandoned by his biological parents at some point in his past? The Bible doesn't tell us. In fact, we know more about David's relationships with Saul and Jonathan than about the relationships within his own family. However, a few things we do know. David was the youngest child, and while his older brothers went off on their adventures, he was the baby brother left behind to tend the sheep. When the prophet Samuel asked to meet Jesse's sons, David's father didn't consider him worthy of mention. No wonder David feared being left out of the family circle. If David's own father devalued him, what if his heavenly Father had done likewise?

God's promise of presence

How do we picture our heavenly Father? Is He the severe parent who occasionally — even impulsively — turns away from us, leaving us to wallow in our feelings of rejection? As you ponder these questions, review the following biblical promises, and consider what they reveal about God's nature and His intentions:

Be robust and courageous. Do not be afraid or terrified because of them, for the Lord your God goes with you; he will never leave you nor forsake you. (Deuteronomy 31:6)

For the sake of his great name the Lord will not reject his people, because the Lord was pleased to make you his own. (1 Sam. 12:22)

These don't sound like descriptions of a captain about to jump ship. Nor is this an exasperated parent on the verge of giving up on a wayward child. No, this is our Divine Captain, our Perfect Parent, pledging never to abandon His loved ones.

Before we draw any conclusions about God the Father, we should reconsider our assumptions about Him. Do we regard Him as a stern, patriarchal figure? Or is He softer — perhaps even maternal — in nature? To a significant degree, our image of God influences our sense of intimacy with Him.

God's parental gender

We can't avoid the fact that the Bible uses masculine imagery when speaking about God. This is, in part, because of the authors' cultural milieu and for the sake of linguistic efficiency. But God is beyond, and not limited to, the gender distinctions "He" has created. God is neither male nor female but, in some mysterious way, may be both. Intriguingly, when Scripture speaks of divine attributes like grace, love, and mercy, the imagery is often feminine. There is a degree of gender balance in the adjectives used to describe the various aspects of God. Given this, seeing God as our just and righteous Father *and also* our kind and gentle Mother expands our understanding of the divine character.

Listen to Isaiah 49:15-16: *"Can a mother forget the baby at her breast and have no compassion on the child she has borne? Though she may forget, I will not forget you! See, I have engraved you on the palms of my hands; your walls are ever before me."* These are not the words of a Father with clenched fists. Instead, the imagery is that of a nursing Mother with a baby nestled in Her caring hands. At times God may seem like an angry Father, but on other occasions He is a loving Mother protecting Her child.

This much is clear: God is never a negligent or absentee Parent. He (or She) is the essence of the perfect Parent who is attentive and caring at all times. *All* times.

Feelings of eternal abandonment

Many people have never experienced genuine familial love from parents or siblings, and perhaps not even from their spouses or their own children. As sad as this is, these are human relationships, and human relationships are subject to human failings. But God is not so easily put off by human behavior. He understands our brokenness and shortcomings. No matter how insecure we may feel, God never averts His gaze from us. As I've said, our feelings are fickle, so we should be hesitant to trust them. However, God is utterly trustworthy and not subject to fickle emotions. His love for us never fades or disappears. Not in this life, nor in the life to come.

David writes, *"I remain confident of this: I will see the goodness of the Lord in the land of the living."* (Ps. 27:13) This "land of the living" is where we exist right now. God is actively attending to us in this present dimension and in our eternal future as well. Paul's own experience confirms this: *"We are hard pressed on every side, but not crushed; perplexed, but not in despair; persecuted, but not abandoned; struck down, but not destroyed. We always carry around in our body the death of Jesus, so that the life of Jesus may also be revealed in our body."* (2 Cor. 4:8-10) Even when we are at our lowest, we are never out of God's care, and we are never out of His heart.

The lost boy

Remember the lost boy at the beginning of the chapter? When we left him, he was alone on the ground sobbing. Here's the rest of the story. As you may have guessed, I was that boy. It was the first time I had experienced feelings of abandonment, and it's a memory that will never leave me. My palms are sweating as I write about it 60 years later. Fortunately, the story has a happy ending.

Well, sort of.

In the midst of my despair in the park outside the art museum that day, I suddenly heard my father calling my name. I looked up and saw Dad running towards me. You can imagine the joy and relief I felt in being reunited with my father and the rest of my family. Sheer elation!

If I wanted to put a fairy tale spin on my story, I would end it right here. But there's more. My father was a tough guy. A *real* tough guy. He didn't sweep me into his arms, hug and kiss me, then carry me home. The world of my childhood was less than perfect. What Dad did was grab the back of my neck and drag me back to rejoin the family, scolding me all the way. He was determined to teach me a lesson about wandering off. There was no tender, protective embrace. But that was okay. Simply being back in the company of my father and family was comfort enough. I discovered there is something far worse than being reprimanded by my father, and that is feeling *abandoned* by my father.

As I look back now, I realize that my dad was probably more upset with himself than with me. I'm now a father myself, so I know how such things feel to a parent. A son losing his father is one thing, but it doesn't compare to what a father feels in losing his son. The next time you feel as if you've lost God, consider how He might be feeling about losing you. His love for us is so passionate that He never wants to lose any of His children.

The bottom line is this: We may lose track of God from time to time, but God never loses track of us. No matter how we feel or what we think, God is the perfect Parent. He's a much better Father — and a much better Mother — than we can imagine or ever be ourselves. He (She) never abandons His (Her) loved ones. And this is a promise worthy of our complete faith. Speaking on behalf of his Father, God's Son gives us this guarantee: *"And surely I am with you always, to the very end of the age."* (Matthew 28:20b) Like Son, like Father.

Some practical steps to consider when you feel abandoned:

• Invite a trusted friend to mentor you, someone capable of understanding your feelings and offering wise and honest counsel.

• Read again and again the Scriptural promises. Become familiar with God's relentless love and constant presence with you. Better yet, commit these promises to memory.

• Become a regular participant in a faith community. A church. A small group. A club. An activity group. A fellowship gathering. Feelings of abandonment are often rooted in feeling sorry for ourselves and they dissipate once we're in the company of those who care for us.

• If you can't shake your despair, seek out a professional counselor or therapist who can help to free you of past hurts, to get to the source of your feelings of abandonment, and to guide you along the path of forgiveness (of self and others) and inner-healing.

• "The last thing you feel like doing is often the first thing you have to do." This has become a motivational axiom I apply daily. As soon as you sense that negativity is immobilizing you, force yourself to take a positive initiative. Stop moaning about your own woes and open your eyes to the needs of others. Consider how you can help them. Don't wait for someone to come to your aid; instead, come to the aid of others. Attend to someone in need.

Additional readings

Have I not commanded you? Be strong and courageous. Do not be afraid; do not be discouraged, for the Lord your God will be with you wherever you go. **– Joshua 1:9**

So do not fear, for I am with you; do not be dismayed, for I am your God. I will strengthen you and help you; I will uphold you with my righteous right hand. **– Isaiah 41:10**

No longer will they call you Deserted, or name your land Desolate. But you will be called Hephzibah, and your land Beulah; for the Lord will take delight in you, and your land will be married.

– Isaiah 62:4

But we have this treasure in jars of clay to show that this all-surpassing power is from God and not from us. We are hard pressed on every side, but not crushed; perplexed, but not in despair; persecuted, but not abandoned; struck down, but not destroyed. We always carry around in our body the death of Jesus, so that the life of Jesus may also be revealed in our body. For we who are alive are always being given over to death for Jesus' sake, so that his life may also be revealed in our mortal body. So then, death is at work in us, but life is at work in you.

– 2 Corinthians 4:7-12

Chapter 2
LONELINESS

"If abandonment is the first blow, loneliness is the second. It is the lethal fallout that lingers long after the blast." **– Richard A. Davis**

"For I am convinced that neither death nor life, neither angels nor demons, neither the present nor the future, nor any powers, neither height nor depth, nor anything else in all creation, will be able to separate us from the love of God that is in Christ Jesus our Lord."
– Romans 8:38-39

"All great and precious things are lonely." **– John Steinbeck, *East of Eden***

Katie stood before the mirror putting the finishing touches on her make-up. Anyone else would have admired the 17-year-old's beauty, but Katie saw only empty eyes staring back at her. She adjusted her skirt, smoothed her sweater, and surveyed her bedroom, going through the motions but feeling nothing. Seeing that everything was neat and in order, Katie stepped out and closed the door behind her. She kissed her mother goodbye and departed.

Katie followed the plan she had devised months before. She rode her mother's bicycle to an isolated spot less than a mile from her home, climbed off, and leaned the bike against a fence. She looked in all directions, checked her watch, and quickly entered the railway tunnel. It was a short walk into total darkness. Katie stopped in the middle of the railroad tracks, took a deep breath, and waited. A few minutes later Katie heard the metallic roar of the approaching train and felt the ground tremble. The last thing she saw was the blinding glare of the headlights before the engine hit her.

Lethal loneliness

I officiated at Katie's funeral. Her mother was a member of our church, so I was called upon to minister to the family in the dark days following Katie's suicide. It wasn't the first time I had attended to a family in the wake of suicide, nor would it be the last. Every suicide brings with it indescribable pain and unanswerable questions. And loneliness is almost always a contributing factor. While Katie's terrible tale may seem rare, such incidents are far more frequent than one might imagine. Teenage suicide among young people today is increasing at an alarming and unprecedented rate. Recent studies show that loneliness is a common precursor in suicides and homicides worldwide. And while loneliness is rarely listed as the cause of death, it is often a silent accomplice.

In Katie's case, the gruesome suicide left those who knew her wondering how such a gentle, bright, and attractive young woman could have made such a fatal decision. However, as the clues started to come together, it became clear that Katie had been slowly and silently sinking into a state of emotional isolation. What began as inner sadness turned into depression, with even her closest friends being unaware of what was happening. She started to think she had no real friends. Her parents' divorce and her sister's move to another city contributed to Katie's feelings of despair. No one understood her. No one cared. Hers was an existence of solitary confinement. So intense was her inner pain that she had come to believe that only death could bring relief.

While loneliness is not listed as a leading threat to public health, it may, in fact, be the most prevalent and pernicious of killers. It's an invisible enemy that has targeted humanity since the beginning, and, like a sinister predator, it stalks its prey with such stealth that it often isn't detected until it's too late. Its modus operandi isn't a bullet, razor blade, bottle of pills, or speeding train; it is the silent suffocation of the soul.

24

In the previous chapter, we discussed abandonment. When a person feels abandoned, he or she becomes susceptible to the lingering gloom of loneliness. And while it rarely results in the desperate escape Katie chose, it imposes a heavy toll nonetheless.

When normal loneliness becomes abnormal

I confess that loneliness is not something I have often experienced firsthand. I've had occasional pangs of what I would consider "normal" loneliness, but, thankfully, I have not suffered the feeling of utter isolation so many others have. However, I do listen carefully when those I counsel describe it. Fortunately, I enjoy my own company enough that being alone doesn't frighten or threaten me. Having grown up in a large family and rarely being alone, I've had no trouble learning to savor my alone time as an adult. Still, I know the risks of loneliness are real, and one need not have suffered loneliness to feel compassion for those who do.

So, if our concern here is not "normal" loneliness, what is it? Let's start with a definition. I found this description of loneliness posted on the internet (with no source listed):

"Loneliness is an emotional state in which a person experiences a powerful feeling of emptiness and isolation. It is more than the feeling of wanting company or wanting to do something with another person. It is a feeling of being cut off, disconnected and/or alienated from other people so that it feels difficult or even impossible to have any form of meaningful human contact. Lonely people often feel empty or hollow inside. Feelings of separation or isolation from the world are common amongst those that are lonely."

Some of our greatest thinkers have attempted to describe the loneliness that descends upon the human soul when one feels alone. Thomas Wolfe wrote, *"The whole conviction of my life now rests upon the belief that loneliness, far from being a rare and curious phenomenon, peculiar to myself and to a few other solitary men, is the central and inevitable fact of human existence."*

The saintly and often solitary Mother Teresa once said, *"Loneliness and the feeling of being unwanted is the most terrible poverty."*

Author Joseph Conrad made this observation: *"Who knows what true loneliness is — not the conventional word, but the naked terror? To the lonely themselves it wears a mask. The most miserable outcast hugs some memory or some illusion. Now and then a fatal conjunction of events may lift the veil for an instant. For an instant only. No human being could bear a steady view of moral solitude without going mad."*

The tormented genius Vincent Van Gogh wrote these words shortly before shooting himself: *"One may have a blazing hearth in one's soul, and yet no one ever comes to sit by it."* Loneliness in the extreme produces fear so unbearable that it can drive a person to take his own life.

Imagine throwing a party and inviting all your friends and family, but no one shows up. You clean the house, cook a big meal, set the table, put on your best clothes, pour the drinks, stoke the fire, and then you wait. And wait. And wait some more. But the doorbell never rings. I know people who feel like this describes their entire life. No one knows them. No one thinks about them. No one understands them. No one cares what happens to them. No one loves them.

Songs for lonely people

In 1974, the pop group America had a number one hit called *Lonely People*. Here are the lyrics:

This is for all the lonely people,
Thinking that life has passed them by;
Don't give up until you drink from the silver cup,
And ride that highway in the sky.

This is for all the single people,
Thinking that love has left them dry;
Don't give up until you drink from the silver cup,
You never know until you try.
Well, I'm on my way,
Yes, I'm back to stay.
Well, I'm on my way back home.

The late Dan Peek—a self-confessed lonely person himself—
co-wrote *Lonely People* with his wife as a celebration of their love
and a declaration of Peek's liberation from personal melancholy.
The song urges those caught up in despair to hang in there until
their thirsty soul is quenched and they find their way "back
home." It is a wishful thought, but it takes more than lyrical pep
talk to rescue someone from an emotional pit. A spiritual
transformation and renovation of the personality is required.

The Bible has plenty of songs for lonely souls. Isaiah 41:8-13
and Psalm 46 are good examples. The prophet Isaiah offers these
words to lonely people: *"I have chosen you and have not rejected you.
So do not fear, for I am with you; do not be dismayed, for I am your God.
I will strengthen you and help you; I will uphold you with my righteous
right hand."* The psalmist adds his own refrain: *"God is our refuge
and strength, an ever-present help in trouble. Therefore we will not fear,
though the earth give way and the mountains fall into the heart of the
sea, though its waters roar and foam and the mountains quake with their
surging."* Both songs resonate with the same theme. Our problem
isn't being alone; it's the *fear* of being alone.

Why is it that two people can be alone and one seems
thoroughly content while the other is agitated and restless? Why
is one person's quiet retreat another person's tortuous isolation? It
may be because our outward situation does not necessarily
determine our emotional condition. Imagine two prisoners in the
same cellblock. One finds peace in his confinement while the
other sinks into despair and hangs himself. Their incarceration is
the same, but their mindsets are starkly different. How can this
be? Based on Isaiah, Psalms, and other biblical passages, it's all
about our internal disposition rather than our external situation.

Jesus, solitary man

Jesus was often alone. But was he ever lonely? We know his unique nature set him apart from the rest of us. In a sense, he had no peers. There was no "Messianic Fellowship" to surround him with support. Jesus had no earthly mentors or true equals. But we do know this. When he felt weary and stressed out, he physically withdrew from others in order to be alone. Herein is the paradox. While his divine identity set him apart from those around him, he was never truly alone because he was aware that his heavenly Father was constantly with him. That seems to have been all the companionship he needed.

Of course, we are not Jesus. And yet, his behavior under stress shows us that our emotional stability is not dependent on others. Jesus demonstrates that we have access to an inner peace that transcends outer turmoil.

Divine compensation for loneliness

In the 14th chapter of the Gospel of John, Jesus teaches his disciples a lesson about fear and loneliness just hours before his arrest. In verses 18-20, he makes this cryptic promise: *"I will not leave you as orphans; I will come to you. Before long, the world will not see me anymore, but you will see me. Because I live, you also will live. On that day you will realize that I am in my Father, and you are in me, and I am in you."* If Jesus knew he would soon be separated from his friends, why did he promise never to abandon them? In a matter of hours, he would be dead, so how was he going to stay with them? Either he was delusional, or there's more going on here.

Notice that Jesus' promise to remain with his disciples came with conditions. To experience his presence, the apostles would have to do something. Look at verse 15. *"If you love me, keep my commands."* This instruction precedes the promise. *If* Jesus' disciples keep his commandments, he will send them a "Comforter." This conditional promise is repeated several times.

In verse 21, Jesus says that whoever hears his commands and obeys them will experience God's presence. Hearing this, Judas (not Judas Iscariot but the other Judas) asks Jesus what this means, and the Lord replies, *"Anyone who loves me will obey my teaching. My Father will love them, and we will come to them and make our home with them. Anyone who does not love me will not obey my teaching."* Jesus couldn't have spoken more clearly. God will dwell among—even within—those who obey His Son...*if* they internalize His Word and live by it. By implication, this same promise is given to everyone who does likewise today.

Loneliness and trust

The Bible makes a correlation between our lonely feelings and our refusal to trust in and obey God's Word. At first glance, this sounds more like law than grace, since it seems to imply that the lonely person is, at least in part, guilty of causing his own suffering. But that isn't what Scripture says.

Whenever the Bible addresses the issue of loneliness and pain, it makes a distinction between loneliness and self-pity. Aloneness isn't the problem; it's that we need to learn how to be alone and grow from it.

When it comes to loneliness—and most things in life—attitude is everything. The complainer thinks, "Because I am alone, there must be something wrong with me. Why doesn't someone call me? Am I unlovable, or even bad? I must have done something wrong, and whatever it is has caused God to place me in isolation. This is what I deserve. Poor me!" Compare this to the attitude of those who have invited God to accompany them in their aloneness. Their thinking is: "God loves me. He has invited me into an intimate relationship with Him and gives me uninterrupted time in His presence. This is a gift that renews my strength and keeps me healthy." Right attitudes flow from right thinking.

Blaming others for our loneliness

Being told that we must take responsibility for our own emotional disposition is something many of us don't want to hear. Dr. Mark Evans of the University of Oregon Counseling Center says: *"Growing up in a society that promotes a dependence upon, or even an addiction to external things for a sense of well-being — food, clothes, drugs, other people — leaves many of us floundering when left all to ourselves. Some of us may have internalized the false view that to be happy is to be surrounded by others at all times, regardless of how we may feel in their company."*

I think Dr. Evans is on to something. We are indeed inclined to blame others for our problems. If our lives aren't working, we think it must be someone else's fault. *"They* are wrecking my life. *They* are affecting my mood. I am innocent, and *they* are guilty." Such an attitude causes us to search for a magic bullet to put things right. A good lawyer. A doctor. A therapist. A fix-it book. A seminar or program. A support group. Whether we admit it or not, we believe what we need most is someone — or several someones — to show us sympathy and to love us the way we think we deserve to be loved.

If we don't get the attention we crave, we start to blame others for our loneliness. "It's their problem, not ours. They are emotionally handicapped. No wonder they can't meet our needs." When we blame others for our emotional state, it never ends well.

Dr. Evans continues, *"If we can learn to be truly intimate with ourselves, then we are never alone. This sort of intimacy, however, is not always easy to come by. It may take facing the wounded, deficient parts of ourselves, as well as the wonderful, abundant parts. In many families such parts were rejected and denied, and therefore went underground, perhaps festering into a low-grade depression."*

I assume Dr. Evans has been trained in behavioral therapy, so it's not surprising that his solution for loneliness involves a methodical reprogramming of our damaged self-esteem.

No doubt this is helpful to many—even those who don't suffer the torment of loneliness, but there is something more—something practical—that we can do. And it's less expensive and more liberating than psychotherapy. It is, in fact, the supreme solution.

Taking responsibility

What is this supreme solution? It is learning to examine ourselves in the light of Christ and allowing that light to bleach out our inner stains. When we ask God to show us the sins we cling to, He ends up showing us the sins that cling to us. And usually they are sins we don't know are there. What are the hurts and resentments we refuse to hand over to God? Strangely enough, there may be things we hold on to because they bring us the attention and sympathy we crave. Our bitter complaining generates negative attention, and that provides us with a measure of perverse satisfaction. This sounds bizarre until we realize that *negative attention* is, for many, better than *no attention at all.*

Sadly, the longer we remain bitter, the less likely it is that we will get better. By alienating others with our constant negativity and complaining, we end up reducing our capacity to accept genuine love when it is finally offered, whether by others or by God. Potential caregivers are repelled by our super-sensitivity and prickliness, which form an impenetrable shield around us. As the old saying goes, "it's hard to hug a porcupine."

If my general demeanor is that of a malcontent, I am building relational walls rather than bridges. And my walls are so thick and my barbed wire so sharp that people can no longer get near me. It appears that I prefer moodiness and broodiness instead of companionship and community. The only vibes I send out are toxic and off-putting. I might as well wear a signboard saying, "Stay away. I am high maintenance!" Consciously or subconsciously, I announce to one and all that I choose to live in a lonely fortress rather than the hospitable habitat God has for me.

Self-esteem and God-esteem

Few things break a parent's heart more than seeing a child so bereft of self-esteem that no amount of praise and reassurance has any effect. Children who believe they don't deserve love refuse to accept love, and they risk spending a lifetime in the solitary confinement that I described earlier. They fall into habitual self-deprecation and can no longer squelch the negative thought patterns to open the channels that carry messages that affirm and nurture.

The God of the Bible never abandons us or allows us to stray beyond His reach. He proclaims His desire for us from the moment of our creation, saying, "This one is good. Very good. This child is beautiful." All of Scripture attests to how our Creator cherishes our company, and this is something far superior to peer-generated or self-generated esteem.

The Apostle Paul asks a fundamental question in Romans 8:31b: *"If God is for us, who can be against us?"* This rhetorical question provides great assurance to anyone who questions his or her worth. Not only are we never alone, the Ruler of the universe is our ally, defender, and constant companion.

Marinate in this promise. No matter how you feel, or what you think of yourself, you are deeply and thoroughly loved by the One who made you. And nothing in the universe can change that. This love is pervasive and powerful enough to evaporate the fear of isolation.

Our lives are so enveloped in our Creator's care and compassion that we are never alone. Not in this life, nor in the next. Once you accept and believe this, you will no longer be tormented by feelings of loneliness.

Suggested remedies for loneliness:

- **Engage in an ongoing dialogue with God.** As believers, we have the privilege of hosting the Holy Spirit within our soul. Take advantage of that. Go on a daily walk and invite

God's Spirit to accompany you. There are several ways to do this. Bring your iPod and listen to devotional podcasts as you walk. Offer thought-prayers in rhythm with your pace. As you encounter people along the way, imagine God's love for them and silently pray for them. Better yet, smile and greet them. You may eventually feel comfortable initiating conversation with them. Physical activity stimulates mental activity, and this, in turn, stimulates spiritual activity. I have been taking these spiritual walks for many years — for 60-90 minutes (or about five miles) every day. It's a discipline that strengthens my body, mind, and spirit simultaneously.

- **Examine your intentions and change your thought patterns as necessary.** Loneliness is a choice. Our feelings follow our choices and are not real themselves. Since our physical situation need not determine our state-of-mind, we can choose *not* to be lonely. If you often feel lonely, it may be because you've allowed your emotions to dictate your mood. Instead of following your emotions, give your behavior (actions) leadership over your emotions. If you feel lonely and then act lonely, things will only get worse. However, if your demeanor is outgoing and inviting, you will attract and more freely engage with others — and others will engage with you — and you will no longer feel alone. Do not wait for others to come to your rescue. They won't. Focus on those who may need *your* help.

- **Take initiative and use your imagination.** Discover what you really enjoy. Sports. Art. Conversation. Nature. Music. Find a hobby. Get in touch with your passions, and then join others who share that passion. *A community of shared interests will help you develop an optimistic attitude.* Whether it's a club, organization, church, or informal gathering of likeminded friends, it will draw you out of yourself. And if you can't find anything to fill your needs, start something. You'll be amazed at how people come out of the bushes when something (or someone) attractive appears.

- **Evaluate your mental diet and adjust your activities.** Just as we are what we eat, we also are what we consume mentally. For some odd reason, when we're depressed, we are drawn to things that feed our depression. Take inventory of what you are reading, watching on TV, listening to, and thinking about. Are these things building you up or tearing you down? Negative *input* produces negative *output*. Change your mental diet to include spending more time with positive people and reading (even memorizing) Scripture and other inspirational literature. View uplifting and edifying TV shows, movies, and websites. Add creative activities to your daily schedule. Paint. Write. Make music. Pray. Decorate your home. Take on a project. Phone a friend. Remember that action alters mood.

- **Devote yourself to living positively every day.** Your first activity every morning should be positive. Don't watch the news or read the newspaper immediately after waking up. It's usually bad news. Start the day with something enjoyable. A walk in the woods. A cup of coffee. A short reading from the Bible. A time of silent meditation and relaxation. Welcome each new day with optimism. Before you begin your daily activities, make a list of tasks you want to accomplish that day, and then check off each task as it is completed. Finally, end your day the way it began: on a positive note. Don't watch or read the news before going to bed, and don't try to fall asleep while watching something depressing on TV. Start and end each day positively.

Additional readings

God is our refuge and strength, an ever-present help in trouble. Therefore we will not fear, though the earth give way and the mountains fall into the heart of the sea, though its waters roar and foam and the mountains quake with their surging. There is a river whose streams make glad the city of God, the holy place where the Most High dwells. God is within her, she will not fall; God will help her at break of day.

Nations are in uproar, kingdoms fall; he lifts his voice, the earth melts. The Lord Almighty is with us; the God of Jacob is our fortress. Come and see what the Lord has done, the desolations he has brought on the earth. He makes wars cease to the ends of the earth. He breaks the bow and shatters the spear; he burns the shields with fire. He says, "Be still, and know that I am God; I will be exalted among the nations, I will be exalted in the earth." The Lord Almighty is with us; the God of Jacob is our fortress. **– Psalm 46**

"But you, Israel, my servant, Jacob, whom I have chosen, you descendants of Abraham my friend, I took you from the ends of the earth, from its farthest corners I called you. I said, 'You are my servant'; I have chosen you and have not rejected you. So do not fear, for I am with you; do not be dismayed, for I am your God. I will strengthen you and help you; I will uphold you with my righteous right hand. All who rage against you will surely be ashamed and disgraced; those who oppose you will be as nothing and perish. Though you search for your enemies, you will not find them. Those who wage war against you will be as nothing at all. For I am the Lord, your God, who takes hold of your right hand and says to you, Do not fear; I will help you." **– Isaiah 41:8-13**

"If you love me, keep my commands. And I will ask the Father, and he will give you another advocate to help you and be with you forever – the Spirit of truth. The world cannot accept him, because it neither sees him nor knows him. But you know him, for he lives with you and will be in you. I will not leave you as orphans; I will come to you. Before long, the world will not see me anymore, but you will see me. Because I live, you also will live. On that day you will realize that I am in my Father, and you are in me, and I am in you.

Whoever has my commands and keeps them is the one who loves me. The one who loves me will be loved by my Father, and I too will love them and show myself to them."

Then Judas (not Judas Iscariot) said, "But, Lord, why do you intend to show yourself to us and not to the world?"

Jesus replied, "Anyone who loves me will obey my teaching. My Father will love them, and we will come to them and make our home with them. Anyone who does not love me will not obey my teaching. These words you hear are not my own; they belong to the Father who sent me.

"All this I have spoken while still with you. But the Advocate, the Holy Spirit, whom the Father will send in my name, will teach you all things and will remind you of everything I have said to you. Peace I leave with you; my peace I give you. I do not give to you as the world gives. Do not let your hearts be troubled and do not be afraid.

"You heard me say, 'I am going away and I am coming back to you.' If you loved me, you would be glad that I am going to the Father, for the Father is greater than I. I have told you now before it happens, so that when it does happen you will believe. I will not say much more to you, for the prince of this world is coming. He has no hold over me."

– John 14:15-30

What, then, shall we say in response to these things? If God is for us, who can be against us? He who did not spare his own Son, but gave him up for us all – how will he not also, along with him, graciously give us all things? Who will bring any charge against those whom God has chosen? It is God who justifies. Who then is the one who condemns? No one. Christ Jesus who died – more than that, who was raised to life – is at the right hand of God and is also interceding for us. Who shall separate us from the love of Christ? Shall trouble or hardship or persecution or famine or nakedness or danger or sword? As it is written: "For your sake we face death all day long; we are considered as sheep to be slaughtered." No, in all these things we are more than conquerors through him who loved us. **– Romans 8:31-37**

Chapter 3
DEPRESSION

If we wish to have real wisdom we must know two things: we must know God and we must know ourselves. In order to know one of these properly we must also know the other. – **John Calvin, *The Institutes of the Christian Faith***

I will exalt you, Lord, for you lifted me out of the depths and did not let my enemies gloat over me. Lord my God, I called to you for help, and you healed me. You, Lord, brought me up from the realm of the dead; you spared me from going down to the pit. – **Psalm 30:1-3**

My first personal encounter with depression came in 1984 when I was in my mid-30s and living in Belfast, Northern Ireland. I was serving a church in the heart of the city at a time when the country was embroiled in the heat of "The Troubles."[1] Having moved with Susan and our two young children from the tranquility of the American Midwest, Belfast was a shock to my system. Suddenly tension and terrorism became part of my daily existence. During our time there, we lost friends and church members to roadside bombings, survived the detonation of a thousand-pound IRA car bomb a block away from us, and endured frequent body searches, roadblocks, and building evacuations. We found ourselves trying to cope with the constant anxiety of living in a sectarian war zone. The entire country was in a fog of depression. To make things worse, we had to adjust to the notorious gloom of Northern Irish weather and air pollution. We had only seven days of sunshine during our two years of residency in Ulster. And I'm not exaggerating.

---

[1] "The Troubles" refer to a period of ethnic/religious/political conflict that began in Northern Ireland in the 1960s and continues even today, albeit more sporadically. The principal issues are the constitutional status of Northern Ireland and the relationship between the Protestant (Loyalist) majority and the Roman Catholic (Nationalist) minority. The Troubles have produced violence and political and military (or paramilitary) conflict.

We experienced the worst stretch of dismal weather on record. Twenty-four miserable months of wet and cold! Irrespective of The Troubles, the unrelenting dampness and darkness brought with it an inner gloom so heavy that I could barely summon the will to climb out of bed each morning.

After months of this, enough was enough. I made an appointment to get a complete medical exam. I was convinced there must be a physical cause for my deepening melancholy. But the doctor's findings only made matters worse. He declared that I was strong as an ox! I was devastated. I had hoped they would find something requiring me to stop working and recuperate in bed. No such luck. For the first time in my life, I had to accept that I had a psychological issue and needed to come to terms with the debilitating pain of depression.

Every morning for the next year, I pried open my sleep-deprived eyes to contemplate having to make it through another gloomy day. It was a good news/bad news dilemma. The good news was that the long, awful night was over; the bad news was that I now had to survive another long, awful day. It was like living in a prison cell with no fresh air, no light, and no end in sight. I was surrounded by loving people but had no hope or joy in my life. It felt as if God had abandoned me. My intellect told me He hadn't, but my emotions said otherwise. This is the deceptive game that depression plays in our minds.

What is depression?

The Psalms quote at the beginning of this chapter describes one man's descent into the bottomless pit of depression. Before considering that dark abyss, let's first define our terms. Depression is a word used to describe anything from negative thoughts to a mental/emotional illness so severe that it literally kills its victims. The most common types of psychological depression are:

- situational (or temporary) depression
- clinical depression
- depression as a personality (or mood) disorder

- melancholic depression
- atypical depression
- psychotic depression
- postnatal depression
- physiological depression
- kinesiological depression.

It is not my purpose to analyze each of these categories, so I'll leave that to those who are more qualified. My interest is in viewing depression from a biblical perspective and considering how it saps the soul and deflates the spirit. Because depression is a malady that manifests itself differently from person to person, trying to diagnose and treat it is controversial in medical and religious circles alike. We see this in the many conflicting opinions on the subject. For a more comprehensive study of depression, I suggest you consult other resources. My purpose is to share what I've learned firsthand — and from those I've counseled — about the journey into what Psalm 23 calls "the valley of the shadow of death."

Misery in ministry

Based on my experience, faith offers little, if any, protection against suffering. In fact, in some ways, faith may make us even more vulnerable. Why is this? Because faith sharpens our spiritual senses, making us more susceptible to the visible and invisible dynamics around us. Faith softens the heart, and, unfortunately, life is not easy on soft hearts and tender spirits.

Ironically, I have found that sensitivity can be just as much a liability in ministry as it is an asset. I'm hard-pressed to come up with the name of a prominent Christian leader who hasn't struggled with depression at one time or another. There is evidence that two of the giants of the Reformation, Martin Luther and John Calvin, suffered bouts of depression.

And more than a few theologians and Christian writers and speakers in recent times have experienced this same darkness of the soul.

C.S. Lewis, G.K. Chesterton, Mother Teresa, Billy Graham, Martin Luther King, and thousands of pastors and missionaries have dealt with depression.[2] The size of the list makes us wonder if depression is an actual consequence of ministry. And if it is, we may further wonder how — or even if — God protects His servants from such torment.

The late British pastor and scholar J.B. Phillips devoted himself to translating the King James Bible into modern English in the years following the Second World War. It was while reading *The Phillips New Testament* that I was first captivated by Scripture and drawn closer to Jesus. Years later, I read J.B. Phillips' autobiography and discovered how this gentle churchman had suffered from clinical depression during the last 15 years of his life.

In a revealing and poignant response to one of his correspondents, Phillips wrote:

I think prolonged suffering whether it is mental, physical or both, tends to make us impatient, resentful, angry, and frustrated; we begin to see the jaws of despair. The only value I can see in these experiences is that they do give us more insight and sympathy with the sufferings of others. I never thought, for example, that I should ever know the type of despair that leads people to self-destruction. I know it now, but I am still firmly of the belief that it really solves nothing and is a cowardly gesture.

I think the frightful thing about continual suffering is that it takes the colour and joy out of almost all the proper pleasures of living.

It also, in my case, except for rare intervals, tends to destroy the sense of God.

---

[2] Luther and Calvin's battles against despair and depression have been recounted by many biographers and are also recorded in the Reformers' own personal letters. C.S. Lewis' struggle with inner-darkness is recorded in his candid book *A Grief Observed*. Similar confessions of many prominent Christian leaders, both before and since, are also well documented.

It is no use comparing afflictions; my pains are not your pains or anyone else's. To me it calls for all my inward courage and all my faith in the living God to survive at all. It is really much more than a crumb of comfort to know that whatever we feel God knows all about it. Even when we find it next to impossible to pray I am basically convinced that He understands this too.

There is an almost inescapable loneliness about the experience of prolonged suffering. If we hang on, and of course we must, I am pretty certain that we shall emerge with a far more robust faith. I haven't even begun to "welcome" my afflictions, as St. James suggests in his epistle, but men and women have learned to do this and it must be possible.[3]

The Book of Psalms, a diary of depression

Many of the Bible's leading characters suffered from depression. Abraham. Moses. Elijah. King Saul. Jeremiah. Jonah. Simon Peter. Judas Iscariot. Paul the Apostle. Even Jesus himself. They all seem to have fallen into emotional darkness at one time or another. The biblical figure most associated with depression is King David, whom we believe wrote much of the Book of Psalms. Many of these poems (songs) were birthed in despair, providing us with an intimate record of David's battle against depression.

Those of us who have known depression find in David a kindred spirit. Throughout his life, this shepherd-turned-king repeatedly descended into despondency and bounced back. Psalm 30:3 is an example: *"You, Lord, brought me up from the realm of the dead; you spared me from going down to the pit."* Here is a classic description of depression, and it is a recurring theme throughout the psalms.

Let's explore David's depression.

---

[3] *The Price of Success, An Autobiography* by J. B. Phillips, Harold Shaw Publishers, Wheaton, Illinois, 1984, pp. 213-214.

As a young man, he served in the household of the mentally disturbed King Saul, whose infamous moods swung from adoring David to abhorring him. We can only imagine what effect the king's depression had on the young man destined to become his successor. Perhaps David's exposure to Saul's dark moods contributed to his own emotional swings and moral lapses later on. David's sexual lust caused him to commit adultery with Bathsheba and have her husband Uriah killed. How could this bright and sensitive minstrel/hero/king bear the guilt of his horrendous deeds?

A short while later, David is emotionally devastated when he discovers that his sins have contributed to the death of his infant son. And years after that, David suffers the betrayal of one son and the bloody death of another. What toll did these blows take on this God-fearing and sensitive man? So severe were the wounds in David's soul that he tore his garments to shreds and blasted God, pleading with the Almighty to relieve his agony. The Psalms are David's diary of depression.

Psalm 30:5, with its timeless imagery, is particularly poignant. David writes: *"...weeping may stay for the night, but rejoicing comes in the morning."* This verse captures the dread that so often comes in the middle of the night when a depressed soul is tortured by insomnia or overwhelmed with guilt, grief, and anxiety. Many of us have wallowed in that dark pit ourselves.

The 16th-century Spanish priest, poet, and mystic, Saint John of the Cross, experienced this nocturnal distress and described it as "the dark night of the soul." While depression remains all day, the most severe assault comes at night when it unleashes a barrage of anxiety and the illusion of isolation. While sunrise may bring some relief, it is merely a brief respite. Each new day brings with it the same old pain. Based on my experience, if there is any respite at all from depression, it usually comes in the late afternoon or early evening when the pressures of the day briefly subside. But just hours away, another dark night is lurking.

Isaiah, a wounded healer

Included on my list of Scripture's despondent souls is the Old Testament prophet Isaiah. In Isaiah 40, we find the godly visionary admitting to feeling "faint, weary, powerless, and exhausted." And yet, he must still minister to a community of depressed people and assure them of God's patience and goodness. He writes, "*[The Lord] has sent me to bind up the brokenhearted, to proclaim freedom for the captives and release from darkness for the prisoners, to proclaim the year of the Lord's favor and the day of vengeance of our God, to comfort all who mourn, and provide for those who grieve in Zion — to bestow on them a crown of beauty instead of ashes, the oil of joy instead of mourning, and a garment of praise instead of a spirit of despair. They will be called oaks of righteousness, a planting of the Lord for the display of his splendor. They will rebuild the ancient ruins and restore the places long devastated; they will renew the ruined cities that have been devastated for generations.*" (Isaiah 61:1-4)

Isaiah gets it! In the midst of his own despair, he experiences a mysterious but very real outpouring of divine compassion within his troubled soul. Isaiah 40:31 says, "*Those who hope in the Lord will renew their strength. They will soar on wings like eagles; they will run and not grow weary, they will walk and not be faint.*" The wind beneath Isaiah's wings is not a gentle breeze of human emotion; it is a supernatural jet stream.

As depression descends, those who suffer become increasingly willing to try anything or everything to be cured. We summon what little strength we have left to try to resist the darkness with sheer willpower. If this doesn't work — and it rarely does — we reach out for any "quick fix" that's available. When none of this works, the depression only deepens, leaving us feeling powerless and condemned to endure a life devoid of meaning. The dreadful silence that accompanies depression may eventually cause us to question God's very existence. And even if we are able to cling to the hope that God exists, we don't feel His love and start to resent Him for failing to rescue us.

In my opinion, the greatest obstacle to trusting in God is human pride. Pride imprisons our ego and denies access to anyone who offers help, *especially* to God. Why is this? Perhaps it's because we believe the lie that we can fix whatever is broken within us on our own. Once we think we don't *need* God, we don't *heed* God. A stubborn spirit that resists divine assistance rises within us. Thankfully, it doesn't end here. God, in His grace and patience, waits us out. Even when our lives are woeful, God remains wonderful.

In the midst of our suffering and stubbornness, God intervenes and softens us. He expands our capacity to absorb the compassion of the caring souls around us. More than that, as depression bends us low, God liberates us from self-absorption and opens our eyes to the suffering of others. Remember how J.B. Phillips explained it: *"The only value I can see in [suffering] is that [it gives] us more insight and sympathy with the sufferings of others."* It is nothing short of miraculous that, in the midst of our own pain, God keeps us from slipping into self-pity and instills within us the gift of compassion. Here is the mercy of God. He mends our broken hearts while, at the same time, transforming us into healers for others. We who are wounded become His wounded healers. This is something that psychology and pharmaceuticals alone cannot do.

Secular therapy vs. Christ-based therapy

I have devoted my career to the study of both God's nature and human nature, and I have found there is no better "laboratory" than a church for trying to figure out what makes people tick. I know some Christians—especially among the most conservative—are suspicious of anyone who mixes psychology with theology, seeing this as un-Christian or even anti-Christian. They are convinced that God, and God alone, is all that's needed to maintain mental and emotional health. I believe this is shortsighted in that it creates a false conflict between two disciplines that are complementary in helping people heal and thrive.

Psychology is a valuable tool for examining the thought patterns and habitual behaviors that inhibit our growth. As a science, psychology is not purely empirical (as if any science is), but when it is practiced responsibly and competently, psychology enables self-examination and opens the way for inner-transformation. Isn't this also a Christian goal? And shouldn't it be a goal of all religions? Be wary of those who fan the flames of false conflict between faith and science.

That said, we should acknowledge that there are versions of psychology and clinical therapy that divert people away from Christ. A balanced Christian approach to mental health helps us to engage with God's Spirit by inviting Christ to walk beside us — even *inside* us — to guide us out of our inner darkness and into the light of faith, hope, and love. We should be suspicious of any psychological approach, secular or faith-based, that only turns us inward but never outward.

Most psychotherapeutic approaches involve processing the patient's past and trying to discover how these experiences inhibit the desired changes. The assumption is that self-understanding leads to self-determination, which, in turn, enables the patient to focus his or her energy and efforts on replacing old thought and behavior patterns with new ones. The therapist provides the guidance, but the patient must do the work.

Christ-centered "therapy" follows much the same pattern but adds the spiritual dimension. Those being treated (or counseled) are taught how to: (1) focus on the model of Christ, (2) study the Scriptures for self-understanding, and (3) accept and embrace the healing power of God's Spirit. This process includes learning how to experience God's love and allowing Him to influence our lives. Once we discover we are not alone in our struggles, healthy changes happen.

God provides a real, transcendent strength to overcome the worldly and otherworldly powers around us. This supernatural strength compensates for our natural weaknesses and limitations.

While secular therapies view the self as the primary source of healing, faith-based therapies believe that lasting healing comes from God working within us. The former depends on *our* willpower, while the latter taps into *God's* higher power.

Thankfully, there are many counselors and therapists who understand that the best healing occurs when the mind, body, and spirit are taken seriously and treated together. With so many incompetent options out there, finding the right therapist can prove challenging. Choose carefully!

Theo-therapy

If we fall into depression, how can Christian theology help? First, we need to accept that we are not alone. God sees our suffering, feels it personally, and responds by bringing us into His compassionate embrace. This embrace may be invisible or intangible, but it is very real. Second, we can rest assured that God's companionship and comfort are available even before the healing is complete.

Consider 2 Corinthians 1:3-5: *Praise be to the God and Father of our Lord Jesus Christ, the Father of compassion and the God of all comfort, who comforts us in all our troubles, so that we can comfort those in any trouble with the comfort we ourselves receive from God. For just as we share abundantly in the sufferings of Christ, so also our comfort abounds through Christ.*

In this passage, Paul expands on the lessons of David and Isaiah by commending to us the ultimate Counselor, Jesus Christ. He is the one *"who comforts us in all our troubles,"* enters into our suffering, and brings us consolation. A competent Christian therapist connects his/her patients to a transcendent power capable of providing ongoing physical/emotional/spiritual healing for even the worst internal pain.

When Christ is engaged in our healing, our capacity to endure the pain increases dramatically.

Faith-based therapies—in combination with effective clinical techniques—bring a dimension to the healing process that other approaches lack: they address the patient's spirit, as well as his/her mind and body.

The idolatry of self-determination

In the midst of my own bouts of depression, some of my friends have tried to cheer me up. They urged me to think positive thoughts, count my blessings, and put more effort into my spiritual walk. They suggested that I read the Bible more, pray harder and longer, and get more involved in ministering to others. This may sound good, but it's rarely helpful. I know my friends' intentions were pure, but their advice only made things worse by implying that I was contributing to my own depression. I'm not denying that this may have been partially true—just as it was with King David—but culpability isn't a cure. Being told that we've done something wrong—or haven't done enough right—is like pouring salt in a wound.

The God of the Bible does not heap shame and blame upon our despair. Nor does He throw rules and laws at us. Rather, God provides the assurance that He will attend to us and assist in moving us forward. Misguided spiritual cheerleaders and peddlers of positive thinking are, at best, naive, and, at worst, idolaters. Why do I say this? It's because they put their trust in the power of human potential rather than the power of God. As I've said, this is one of the shortcomings of secular therapists. They believe that we have the power to fix ourselves. And once we adopt a new mental paradigm and apply the right techniques—Bingo!—our healing is complete.

Could it be that God, on occasion, may actually use the pain of depression to deepen and strengthen us? I believe this is not only possible; it is probable. Countless persons throughout history have suffered from depression but risen above it to make significant contributions to society.

Some of God's best work has been accomplished through troubled, melancholy souls like King Solomon, Abraham Lincoln, John Adams, Winston Churchill, Leo Tolstoy and countless others. These individuals suffered depression but didn't let it define them or deter them from doing good. Imagine that. Inspiring acts produced in the midst of despair! I am not suggesting that depression is something to be emulated or celebrated. That would be foolish. But suffering may not be the curse we think it is. Even the worst suffering has produced some of the world's greatest blessings.

Too often, our tendency is to panic when we start to feel blue, which has given birth to multibillion-dollar industries built on the promise of alleviating our pain. People today will spend their last dollar, or swallow any pill, in hopes of avoiding or reducing pain. But what if doing so muffles the voice of God? What if pain is one of God's ways of prompting us to make necessary changes? C.S. Lewis described pain as a "megaphone"[4] God uses to get our attention. We must learn to listen for God's whispers when the drone of depression sets in. A divine whisper can resonate like thunder in a wounded soul. Don't run from pain; just listen more carefully.

Having looked at depression from several angles, I want to close this chapter by suggesting some practical remedies that have worked for me and for others I've known. An important first step is to carefully analyze the problem. That analysis should lead to application. And application should lead to action. What follows are recommended analysis/application/action steps that may hasten your healing from depression.

---

[4] *The Problem of Pain*, by C.S. Lewis, first published in 1940 and republished by Harper Collins in 2009.

Tools and Techniques for Treating Depression:

An important word of caution:

*If you are feeling depressed, consult a health professional immediately! There are many physical conditions that can cause or contribute to depression, and they must be diagnosed and treated. If you have such a condition, no amount of willpower or wishful thinking will help you. The **first thing** to do is be examined by a doctor. Many avoid this essential first step because they're afraid of hearing bad news. Don't use this as an excuse. Seek the professional help that's available near you. It may solve your problem.*

- **Medications. Treating the symptoms isn't enough; you must also treat the causes.** While there are some who strictly oppose the use of medications in treating depression, I do not agree. When depression is caused by a physiological condition (such as bi-polar disorder or schizophrenia), abnormalities in brain and body chemistry must be treated first and with proven methods as prescribed and administered by a competent physician. In other cases, medications may be used to treat feelings, but often these treatments do not bring a full and lasting healing. Anti-depressants can buy us the time needed to soften the edges of depression by offering temporary relief from the immediate crisis of pain and anxiety. These medications, when conscientiously administered by a qualified physician, can be extremely valuable.

- **A combined treatment of psychotherapy and medication is currently the treatment of choice for depression among mental health professionals.** The American Psychological Association's *Monitor on Psychology* [5] published a compelling article summarizing the research in the area of treating patients with a combination of psychotherapy and

---

[5] *Depression Treatment: Psychotherapy, Medication, or Both?* By John M. Grohol, PSY.D. Website link: http://psychcentral.com/lib/depression-treatment-psychotherapy-medication-or-both/0001521

medication. Their conclusion? People get better faster when combined treatment is used instead of relying on either treatment by itself.

- **Anger can be a primary contributor to depression.** Most mental health experts agree that depression is a mix of two emotions: anger and grief. *Depressed people tend to harbor within themselves unresolved anger and unresolved grief.* If you are depressed, ask yourself this difficult question: "Who am I angry at?" You may not have forgiven a relative or friend for his or her insensitivity or for committing an act of injustice against you. Perhaps you've never aired these feelings of anger, talked them through and worked them out. In some cases, our anger and resentment may be against God. If this is true and we've never addressed it, we may be suffering from "emotional cancer." Like a malignant tumor, anger festers and grows until it is killed...or until it eventually kills its host. Thankfully, confession is like chemotherapy. It clears the mind, heals the heart, and renews the spirit to allow for new growth.

- **Unresolved grief and depression.** Grief isn't restricted to dealing with a physical death; to some degree, it follows any loss. We may grieve such things as growing old, being separated from our children, losing a job, leaving our home country, straying from an emotional comfort zone, struggling with our health, and numerous other things. Once we recognize how these things drag us down and then admit our grief to God and others, the Holy Spirit steps in to strip away the power those pent-up feelings have held over us. Suddenly, our conscience is clear. Just as an overloaded plane can crash and burn at take-off, the same can happen with an overloaded conscience. Thankfully, God can attach eagle's wings to the overburdened hearts placed in His trust, just as Isaiah 40:27-31 says. Once we allow God to lighten our emotional load, those new wings give us flight.

- **Don't fall into the trap of laziness.** One of the first casualties of depression is personal discipline, causing us to suppress motivation and become, to put it bluntly, *lazy*. Feelings of despair make it difficult to summon the strength to get out of bed each morning, shower and eat, go to school or work, exercise, or engage socially. When we're depressed, every effort seems daunting. We can't muster the courage and energy to enter a new day. It's easier to crawl back under the covers. In the midst of my depressions, I've had to force myself to do *everything*. But once I've started to do something, the healing has begun. Tackling a dreaded and long-avoided task brought me emotional relief. It may have been something as simple as conversing with others, going out for a run, or merely completing a domestic chore. It may have taken all of my willpower to get started, but afterward my emotional clouds broke, and there was light. This is why one of my personal mantras is: **The last thing I *want* to do is the first thing I *have* to do.**

- **Don't ever try to tackle depression alone.** Let others help you. Family and friends are your best allies. Join a church. Become part of a support group or home Bible study group. If you're a man, hang out with other men of faith. If you're a woman, stay close to other women of faith. If you're a student, link up with other students who have faith in God and sincerely care for you. Becoming part of a compassionate community brings with it repair for despair.

- **Don't trust your feelings.** I'll say it again. DO NOT trust your feelings! Feelings are fickle. They can be influenced by anything from having eaten a bad meal…to drinking too much…to having a stranger give you a dirty look…to _____ (fill in the blank). All sorts of things — both serious and silly — happen every day, and any of them can throw us off kilter and cause anxiety, making us feel like we're losing control. In fact, the only thing we really *can* control is how we respond to such things. In the same way that a roller coaster causes motion sickness, the ups and downs of everyday life can produce *emotion* sickness. If "the ride" is making you feel sick, get off and regain your bearings. Feelings are not facts.

- **When all else fails, fake it!** Accept that it is not normal to feel good all the time. Moods ebb and flow, but it's possible to ride through those moods without letting them sweep you away. Trust what you know to be true instead of those little lies that flutter in and out of your mind. If you're not feeling good, fake it. Act like you really do feel good. Surprisingly, there is power in pretending. Feelings follow actions just as much as actions follow feelings. Perhaps even more. Imagine that one day you don't feel friendly. Okay. That's unpleasant. But it doesn't mean you can't force yourself to *act* friendly. Even though you may be faking it, you might end up making (or keeping) a friend. Or let's say you don't feel thankful. Shake it off and act as if you are. Force yourself to thank God for the good things in your life, even when you don't feel especially grateful. What's so bad about that?

  While we may not be able to control our moods, we can choose to control our behavior. Sing when you're cynical. Laugh when you're grumpy. Offer security to others even when you are feeling insecure. Be helpful when you feel helpless. Touch others even when you don't want others touching you. You don't have to *feel* it in order to *fake* it. And if you fake it well enough, you may start to feel better. It's one of those small miracles that come with living in obedience to God.

A warning about the enemy

Never forget that we have an enemy who doesn't want us to believe what you are reading here. He is the devil, and his goal is to get us to fall for his lies rather than trust in God's truth.

One of Satan's primary strategies is to divide and conquer. He strives to remove us from community and leave us in isolation. He subtly coaxes us to submit to our own feelings while ignoring the feelings of others, turning our gaze inward rather than outward. If the master deceiver can convince us that we are alone and unloved, we become vulnerable to his diabolical tactic of leading us into the darkness of depression. Satan wants to drag us down and deflate us, as opposed to God, who responds to our despondency by infusing us with faith, hope, and love. Watch out for the enemy. He may not cause our depression, but he is an expert at taking advantage of it for his own purposes.

Depression kills; God fills. With this in mind, listen again to the stunning promise at the end of Isaiah 40: *"Those who hope in the Lord will renew their strength. They will soar on wings like eagles; they will run and not grow weary, they will walk and not be faint."*

This isn't pop psychology. It is the Father's promise to His tired and confused children. If we claim this promise for ourselves and apply it to our thoughts and actions, it works wonders. When my spirit is heavy, and my mind and body are weary, every bump in the road feels like a bottomless chasm. But these are the normal potholes that every person hits along the road of life. We eventually get past them. They may jar us, but they won't destroy us. If we just keep rolling and ride through the bumps, we make progress, and the road ahead becomes smoother.

The best is yet to come

Psychology is a changing science—as are all the sciences—with new therapies and medications being introduced constantly. Each generation uses the best tools available at the time. There's no doubt that more and better treatments will be discovered, but, in the end, these are just tools. **God is the ultimate healer.**

Additional readings

I will exalt you, Lord, for you lifted me out of the depths   and did not let my enemies gloat over me. Lord my God, I called to you for help, and you healed me. You, Lord, brought me up from the realm of the dead; you spared me from going down to the pit.

Sing the praises of the Lord, you his faithful people; praise his holy name. For his anger lasts only a moment, but his favor lasts a lifetime; weeping may stay for the night, but rejoicing comes in the morning.

When I felt secure, I said, "I will never be shaken." Lord, when you favored me, you made my royal mountain stand firm; but when you hid your face, I was dismayed.

To you, Lord, I called; to the Lord I cried for mercy: "What is gained if I am silenced, if I go down to the pit? Will the dust praise you? Will it proclaim your faithfulness? Hear, Lord, and be merciful to me; Lord, be my help."

You turned my wailing into dancing; you removed my sackcloth and clothed me with joy, that my heart may sing your praises and not be silent. Lord my God, I will praise you forever. **– Psalm 30**

Why do you complain, Jacob? Why do you say, Israel, "My way is hidden from the Lord; my cause is disregarded by my God"? Do you not know? Have you not heard? The Lord is the everlasting God, the Creator of the ends of the earth. He will not grow tired or weary, and his understanding no one can fathom. He gives strength to the weary and increases the power of the weak. Even youths grow tired and weary, and young men stumble and fall; but those who hope in the Lord will renew their strength. They will soar on wings like eagles; they will run and not grow weary, they will walk and not be faint. **– Isaiah 40:27-31**

Praise be to the God and Father of our Lord Jesus Christ, the Father of compassion and the God of all comfort, who comforts us in all our troubles, so that we can comfort those in any trouble with the comfort we ourselves receive from God. For just as we share abundantly in the sufferings of Christ, so also our comfort abounds through Christ.

If we are distressed, it is for your comfort and salvation; if we are comforted, it is for your comfort, which produces in you patient endurance of the same sufferings we suffer. And our hope for you is firm, because we know that just as you share in our sufferings, so also you share in our comfort. **– 2 Corinthians 1:3-7**

Chapter 4
ANGER

In your anger do not sin; when you are on your beds, search your hearts and be silent. **– Psalm 4:4**

"In your anger do not sin": Do not let the sun go down while you are still angry, and do not give the devil a foothold. **– Ephesians 4:26**

"Anger is an acid that can do more harm to the vessel in which it is stored than to anything on which it is poured." **– Mark Twain**

Several years ago the Associated Press released the following story:

ST. PAUL, Minnesota – Justin John Boudin may have done his anger management homework, but he apparently didn't learn his lesson. The 27-year-old Minnesota man pleaded guilty to fifth-degree assault charges for losing his temper on the way to class.

According to the criminal complaint, Boudin was waiting at a bus stop in August when he harassed a 59-year-old woman. Witnesses say he yelled, "Why don't you show me some respect?" at the woman. The complaint says when she took out her cell to call the police he punched her in the face. When a 63-year-old man tried to stop him, Boudin hit the man with a blue folder. Then he ran, dropping the folder.

Police were able to track him down using the papers inside, which included his name and his anger management homework. Prosecutors expect at a hearing in May he'll be sentenced to time served, which will be at least 120 days and probation.

Speaking as a Minnesotan, I can assure you that an incident like this is, by no means, typical of my home state.

Given the dark humor of the movie *Fargo* and its portrayal of the Upper Midwest, you should know that we're not all gun-happy, beer-guzzling hunters who cut holes in the ice to catch fish and use wood chippers to solve our problems. Having said that, there is one thing the AP story got right. Unleashed anger can be ugly, not just in Minnesotans, but in any of us.

Anger and fear

No matter how many anger management classes we attend or where we hide, there is no escaping the fallout of rage. Humanity's cauldron of anger has been on a steady boil ever since Cain killed his brother Abel. And many of us may be pots-near-a-boil much of the time. We can only hope that once we boil over there won't be any journalists nearby.

Anger is not a single-faceted emotion. It has numerous sources and manifests itself in many ways. The same might be said of any of the emotions discussed in this book, but it is especially true of anger because it tends to be triggered by other emotions, such as fear, disappointment, jealousy, or feelings of rejection. And, of course, anger is a common response to pain and suffering of any kind.

When anger is ignited by a noxious stimulus, it may be the result of nature, of nurture, or of a combination of the two. Whether it's genetic in origin or a byproduct of brain chemistry, anger is a constant state in certain people, as if they were born angry and then chose anger as their emotional default setting. Just as there are sad souls and cheerful souls, there are also souls that are chronically angry. For reasons known or unknown, it seems that they are always mad. In cases where individuals have been abused or victimized, this is understandable. The deprivation of nurture distorts our nature. In such cases, the abuse—whether physical, sexual, or psychological—reshapes their self-image and personality, leaving their emotion-meter stuck in the red (danger) zone.

I am convinced that anger is one of the two most disruptive human emotions. The other being fear. The close connection between anger and fear has been well documented.

Consider the "fight-or-flight syndrome,"[6] which refers to our instinct either to stay and fight or take flight whenever we feel threatened. The combination of these two volatile emotions brings out the worst in us and can cause irreparable, even tragic, damage. Let's be honest. Asking God to quell anger and calm a fearful heart is to pray for a miracle. Breaking deep-seeded emotional habits is a slow and excruciating process.

Does this mean that *all* anger is bad, wrong, or sinful? Of course not. The Bible does not impose value judgments on human emotions but instead treats them as part of God's design, placed within us before Adam and Eve tasted that nasty piece of fruit. Based on Scripture, anger is not necessarily evidence of an unhealthy, immature, or rebellious spirit. This must be said because there has been some bad teaching in a number of religious circles. No emotion is good or bad. An emotion is a conscious mental reaction that is subjectively experienced as a strong feeling directed at something (or someone) and typically causing changes in physiology, mood, and behavior. Emotions simply happen. They are natural, even instinctive. But volition plays a critical role in any emotional sequence. When emotions arise, we have the power to decide what to do with them. Feelings can't be stopped, but we can learn to control our feelings before they produce damaging results.

Both Psalm 4:4 and Ephesians 4:26 say, *"In your anger do not sin."* As just stated, anger itself is not wrong and shouldn't be judged morally. However, allowing any emotion to generate sin *is* wrong and can have moral consequences.

---

[6] According to the *fight-or-flight response*, animals react to threats with a general discharge of the sympathetic nervous system (called *hyperarousal*), which primes them to either fight or flee. This response has been recognized as the first stage of a general adaptation syndrome that regulates stress responses among vertebrates and other organisms, including humans.

—

Anger is not something we must always suppress or be ashamed of. On the contrary, there are times when healthy anger is necessary and even commendable. There are evils in life that demand a response of righteous anger. For example, those who inflict suffering on others or practice injustice must be met by fury. This is "good anger," in that it provides protection and relief for the victims. Without some measure of justifiable anger, society itself is at risk. I'll say more about this in a moment.

God's "holy" anger

The Bible uses anthropomorphic language to describe God's character, and this includes His "emotions." Anger is one of these emotions, and when the anger is God's, it is always presented as holy or righteous in nature (see Numbers 32:13). Other displays of righteous anger can be seen throughout Scripture in the patriarchs, prophets, and other godly individuals, including Jesus himself. Several times the sweet and gentle Savior becomes the Mad Messiah. Exaggerated and misinterpreted descriptions of God's anger have distorted our perceptions of the Divine and repulsed many, but the biblical texts that attribute something analogous to human anger to the Almighty can't be ignored.

Consider what these biblical statements have in common:
- *Refrain from anger and turn from wrath; do not fret — it leads only to evil.* (Psalm 37:8)
- *Whoever is patient has great understanding, but one who is quick-tempered displays folly.* (Proverbs 14:29)
- *Better a patient person than a warrior, one with self-control than one who takes a city.* (Proverbs 16:32)
- *"In your anger do not sin": Do not let the sun go down while you are still angry...* (Ephesians 4:26)
- *Get rid of all bitterness, rage and anger, brawling and slander, along with every form of malice.* (Ephesians 4:31)
- *Everyone should be quick to listen, slow to speak and slow to become angry, because human anger does not produce the righteousness that God desires.* (James 1:19-20)

These verses confirm that anger is a normal part of our human condition. They also stress the importance of keeping our anger in check. If God calls us to control our emotions, He must give us the power to do so, for the Lord never requires the impossible of us. The fact is, if we don't control our anger, it will control us. This is especially important for followers of Jesus because we are subject to higher standards. It's not that we're better than those who do not profess faith in Christ; it's just that we're expected to behave better and depend on God to help us control our passions.

Anger and the tongue

It is said that our words reveal the contents of our hearts. This is especially true when it comes to how we express anger. Winston Churchill made this observation: "A man is about as big as the things that make him angry." The wordsmith Ralph Waldo Emerson offered his own pragmatic assessment: "For every minute you are angry, you lose sixty seconds of happiness." And the famous comedian Groucho Marx said, "If you speak when angry, you'll make the best speech you'll ever regret." (I love that one!) In each of these quotes, the lesson is the same: when a tongue is inflamed with rage, there's no telling who or what it may burn. Has any emotion done more harm than anger? Not to my knowledge.

I once had a colleague who was bold enough to approach anyone using vulgar language and ask, "Do you *eat* with that mouth?" He certainly made his point. As I listen to the voices around me, it seems that more and more people have taken the advice of the irreverent humorist Mark Twain, who said, "When angry, count to four; when very angry, swear." Unfortunately, so many of us have little restraint when it comes to expressing our anger.

While it's true that anger is neither good nor bad, neither right nor wrong, the better part of the Book of James is devoted to warning us about what happens when we allow anger to use its favorite weapon: the tongue.

James 1:20 gives a tongue-taming lesson in one simple statement: *"Everyone should be quick to listen, slow to speak and slow to become angry, because human anger does not produce the righteousness that God desires."* James is saying that unbridled anger cannot produce what God desires most: righteousness.

Angry words are cheap shots with a high price. They shoot down righteousness and justice.

Anger and justice

What does anger have to do with justice? When we perform acts of bigotry, oppression, greed, cruelty, and other injustices, God's righteous anger is aroused. He yearns (and burns) to set things right. Righteous anger is an appropriate response to wrongdoing. And righteous anger demands justice. If you are committed to working with God for His causes, be prepared to feel some righteous anger yourself.

Righteous anger may help to bring justice, but it can't fix a fallen world. This is something only divine grace can produce. That's why civil rights movements, social action groups, and other compassionate organizations cannot, in and of themselves, save the world, no matter how sincere their intentions may be. Their initiatives may rectify wrongs, but they can't convert the spirit of rebellion within us. Righteous anger imposes just punishment, but it can't redeem the human soul. It takes a divine act of sacrificial love to work that miracle. James implores us to *"get rid of all moral filth and the evil that is so prevalent and humbly accept the word planted in [us], which can save [us]."*

That seed of salvation is the result of Christ's death on the cross. And as it grows within us, it flows into our thoughts, emotions, words, and actions. Before we try to set the world right, we have to make sure our hearts are right.

James urges believers to conform their lives to God's righteous will and resist the *"sordidness and rank growth of wickedness"* (NRSV) or *"moral filth"* (NIV) displayed by the godless. These are strong words for those counted among God's elect. The dictionary defines *sordidness* as "meanly selfish."[7] James knew how mean selfishness sets in whenever a believer mistakes self-righteous anger for righteous anger. When that happens, self-righteous believers of any faith are prone to exhibit ugly anger.

Why do many religious people seem so angry?

Unfortunately, religion and anger too often go hand-in-hand. In recent decades, the religious faith that produces gentleness, generosity, and love has been replaced by the stereotype of sour, dour, and judgmental religious bigotry. I admit that some in the Church—though only a small minority—have fallen far short of biblical standards. This results in God being blamed for the shortcomings of those who carry His name. One only has to study the life of Jesus to see the stark contrast between his teachings and what some people do in his name. Until churchgoers recognize and confess their wrongdoings and change their ways, Christianity, and Christ himself, will be seen as bogus. There are many reasons for the negative public perceptions, but the harshest cynics often are those who have been hurt by religion and want to strike back by venting their bitterness and resentment. Many of those who rant and rave the loudest carry scars of past hurts, real or imagined, inflicted on them in the name of religion. The deeper the pain, the stronger the protest.

Imagine a crowd of hundreds of religious fundamentalists. What is the first image that comes to mind? A festive crowd with happy, smiling faces? A peaceful parade of pacifists? A respectful

---

[7] According to Dictionary.com, "sordid" means: 1. morally ignoble or base; vile. 2. meanly selfish, self-seeking, or mercenary. 3. dirty or filthy. 4. squalid; wretchedly poor and run-down.

and orderly advocacy for reason and compassion? I doubt it. It's more likely you envision an enraged mob shaking their fists and spewing vitriolic diatribes. Why? Because this is the media's depiction of religious zeal: mobs seething with anger and stoked for violence. Whether it is a lone voice or chorus of demonstrators, when religious convictions are expressed with rage and aggression, God's reputation suffers. We project the faces of angry zealots on God, and an enraged face is hard to forget.

In some parts of the world, Muslims are the angry zealots. In other places, Christians or Jews are tainted by rage. Anger mixed with spiritual fervor fuels stereotyping, and no ideology or religion is exempt. Once that stereotype is created, it is easily reinforced. And we know what comes next. Violence.

As religious passions mount, the core message of the faith—which for Christians and Jews is God's love and grace—is lost in the emotional clamor. Unfortunately, the loudest and most offensive voices get the most attention, leaving outside observers to wonder about the nature of the cause. If we don't know any members of the faith personally and have only a superficial understanding of their practices and culture, our perceptions are skewed. The positive message is drowned out by the negativity.

Thankfully, there is a solution. While we cannot control media coverage or public opinion, as Christians, we should consider the image of God we communicate in our words and actions. We must ask ourselves the hard question: "Am I accurately reflecting the God I know and love?" How we answer that question will determine the effectiveness of our public witness. What impression of God's face do people get when they look into ours? Like it or not, demeanor speaks louder than doctrine. Attitude trumps platitude. Enraged voices cannot convey compassion. Our faces reflect the God we extol. The more we know of Jesus, the more of him others should see in us.

Listen again to James: *"Those who consider themselves religious and yet do not keep a tight rein on their tongues deceive themselves, and their religion is worthless."* Oh, the power of that small, pink muscle behind our teeth! Virtually every Scripture dealing with anger calls for the taming of the tongue. Think of the words we have spoken that can never be taken back. The list of my own reckless and hurtful utterances is a mile long. The familiar saying that "sticks and stones may break my bones, but words can never harm me" is poppycock. Not only can words harm, they can destroy. A cut or bruise eventually heals, but a verbal stab in the heart never stops hemorrhaging.

Anger and gender

There's an old joke that asks, "Why is it that whenever a married couple fights they get historical?" (As opposed to *hysterical.*) Marital partners have an uncanny ability to remember their spouse's most hurtful words and then use them later to avenge the hurt.

Wives and husbands have amazing long-term memories when it comes to the verbal wounds they've inflicted on one another. And the volleys are fired both ways. Destructive anger is not a gender issue; it's a *human* issue. Gender roles may account for a higher incidence of angry men verbally abusing women, due to the male pride and machismo, but that doesn't excuse either sex. After reading an early draft of this chapter, a friend who is a psychologist made this astute observation: "That 'men are from Mars, women are from Venus' thing was great for selling books, but it is not an accurate description of the genders. We may socialize genders differently and thus form different modal expressions of anger, but the basic processes of reception and response are the same." (Sounds like a psychologist, right?) Verbal combat is an equal opportunity sport, and any tongue-lashing that wounds a soul violates Scripture and defies the commandment to love. Christ has no part in emotional intemperance.

When it comes to anger, I—like many of us—have had to confront my own inner demons and watch those close to me do the same. This has taught me a few things about emotional volatility. I have compiled these lessons into a collection I will call "Richard's Rules." Even though I have broken every one of these rules myself—some multiple times—that doesn't mean they are not viable. It just means that I'm better at making rules than I am at living up to them. However, I have found that holding higher moral standards than I can live up to keeps me striving for improvement.

Here are Richard's Rules for dealing with anger:

Rule #1: *Do not* let it stew.

Ephesians 4:26 says, *"In your anger do not sin."* Keep this rule and no others are needed. Woven within it are two sub-rules. First, as I mentioned earlier, Scripture does not forbid feeling or expressing any emotion, but it does warn us about the risks in doing so. The healthy expression of anger helps to protect us from the malignancy of emotional repression. Unexpressed anger festering within can cause permanent damage.

Mental health professionals warn us that suppressed anger affects physical health, causing high blood pressure and other illnesses such as depression, personality disorders (i.e., passive-aggressive behavior), chronic cynicism, hostility, and a number of social phobias. We have recently seen an alarming increase in incidents in which individuals overcome by rage have unleashed murderous attacks on classmates, co-workers, family, and innocent victims who happen to be in their line of fire. These are extreme examples, but they show what happens when repressed emotions explode. And even when the carnage is not so obvious, there can be lethal consequences.

The Book of Ephesians advises against letting the sun set on our anger. Sage advice. Unresolved anger is like a dead fish on a hot day. It starts to rot.

Thankfully, my wife Susan and I learned the "solve-it-before-sunset lesson" early in our marriage, and we have tried to live by it for half a century. This has caused us some long, sleepless nights, but it's been worth it. The rule works! Apply it in all your relationships, and I guarantee that you will see positive results. Don't put off till tomorrow what can be defused today.

Rule #2: *Do* let it stew.

My second rule may seem to contradict the first but read on. I think you will see it's complementary rather than contradictory.

In this age of social media, we need to be aware how easily angry impulses can backfire. With instant messaging at our fingertips 24 hours a day, it takes an extra measure of restraint to resist the temptation to vent our emotions impulsively via the electronic media. We should allow our hottest emotions to cool down before they are texted, tweeted, or emailed.

Paul's warning not to let the sun set on our anger is more about preventing resentment rather than rushing reconciliation. When it comes to relational conflict, it's tempting to procrastinate to avoid the discomfort of having to deal with tension directly. That's why Paul advises us to create some space to breathe and cool down. After all, we have until sunset to work things out and that buys us time; not days but at least several hours.

That little buffer of time can make all the difference. Instant messaging erases this buffer and opens the way for regret. Given our technology, we should harness our keypads as well as our tongues. Watch out when emotions are sent at cyber-speed.

How long should we wait before expressing ourselves? I suggest this: wait long enough to allow your itch for a fight to dissipate. That itch is really just an impulsive desire to win, and that's no good. When you're tempted to send an angry message immediately, procrastinate. Allow the sun to descend on the horizon before you do anything. Better yet, delay your response for *several* sunsets.

Test the message before you *text* the message. Knee-jerk reactions are foolish. Generally speaking, the stronger your anger, the longer you should wait. Set the provocation aside, and when you return to it, rethink your *reaction* before acting. Whatever you do, reread your response several times before sending it.

Rule #3: When in doubt, keep your mouth shut.

James 3:1-12 reminds us that unleashed words can't be retracted. The brain must become the master of the tongue. If our mouths fire off thoughts without allowing them to pass through our cognitive filters, we've got a problem. Once that happens, the "beast of blunder" is loosed. The biblical safeguard is found in 2 Corinthians 10:5: *"We take captive every thought to make it obedient to Christ."* Of all the lessons I've learned in life, this verse has had the most impact on my Christian walk and relationships. Learning to mentally restrain thoughts (and feelings) before expressing them is essential to becoming more like Christ. Once we develop this habit of verbal restraint, future regrets are far less likely.

Perfect control over our thoughts is impossible, but I believe we cannot grow spiritually without learning verbal discipline. As soon as thoughts pop into our minds—and I mean *any* thought—we must exercise our God-given power to decide what we will do with them. For me, it works this way. Before I speak or act on a thought, I imagine Jesus endorsing what I am about to say or do.

In light of my faith, are the words I'm about to speak (or the actions I'm about to take) worthy of Christ? If not, I should perish the thought. Kill and demolish it. Perishing the thought is better than allowing that thought to perish other things. Thoughts that punish others deserve to perish.

Rule #4: If you can't cage the beast, get help.

If anger is a recurring problem for you—either as the perpetrator or victim—seek help immediately. Most people with anger issues, if they're honest, know they have a problem.

68

If this is you, seek out a competent person who can help. It may be a professional counselor or therapist, a pastor, a spiritual mentor, or a trusted, mature friend. Whatever you do, don't stop until you have gotten the support you need. Anger is a time bomb, and the longer you wait, the more likely it is to detonate. Disarm it immediately, whatever it takes. For your own sake, and for the sake of your loved ones, make getting help your highest priority.

Rule #5: Create house rules.

Commit yourself to following biblical guidelines whenever someone under your roof is angry. Susan and I agreed before marrying that we would never permit vulgarity in our home. Thankfully, we've been able to keep that promise. No one in our family has ever cursed at another family member. That's not to say we haven't entertained such thoughts; it's just that we haven't given them voice. We've made a family habit of capturing thoughts before speaking. It may seem like a small thing, but it has paid big dividends in maintaining mutual respect and peace within our household.

You may discover other rules for anger protection in your home. Go for it. Make an assessment. What emotional "buttons" do your family members push that hurt or enflame others? What communication patterns have become ruts of rage? Identify them and establish boundaries, making sure every family member agrees to honor those boundaries by never crossing them. Not only is this respectful, it is right in God's eyes. House rules protect households. First lay them out; then play them out.

I want to close this chapter with a word of hope. If you've got an anger problem, it *can* be healed. Change is possible. But first you must surrender your temperament to the scrutiny and management of the Holy Spirit. No tantrum you have thrown, or rage-fueled damage you have done, is beyond God's power to forgive and fix. Your anger may have scared off and turned off everyone in your life, but God has never stopped loving you.

As the old hymn says, Jesus accepts and loves me "just as I am." This is what's so amazing about God's grace. He loves unlovable me...and unlovable you. And knowing that we have the power to tame and control our emotions, we can add a new lyric to the hymn: "God loves me just as I am...but He doesn't want me to stay that way." Our eternity is in God's hands, but as long as we're here we can commit ourselves to the daily task of removing the barriers that separate us from God and from others.

As we dial down our emotional thermostat, we fall to our knees to ask God to forgive our rage-filled past and guide us into a more tranquil future, for that is where the healing happens.

Additional readings

Do not fret because of those who are evil or be envious of those who do wrong; for like the grass they will soon wither, like green plants they will soon die away.

Trust in the Lord and do good; dwell in the land and enjoy safe pasture. Take delight in the Lord, and he will give you the desires of your heart.

Commit your way to the Lord; trust in him and he will do this: He will make your righteous reward shine like the dawn, your vindication like the noonday sun.

Be still before the Lord and wait patiently for him; do not fret when people succeed in their ways, when they carry out their wicked schemes. Refrain from anger and turn from wrath; do not fret — it leads only to evil. For those who are evil will be destroyed, but those who hope in the Lord will inherit the land. A little while, and the wicked will be no more; though you look for them, they will not be found. But the meek will inherit the land and enjoy peace and prosperity. **– Psalm 37:1-11**

A gentle answer turns away wrath, but a harsh word stirs up anger. **– Proverbs 15:1**

"In your anger do not sin": Do not let the sun go down while you are still angry, and do not give the devil a foothold. Anyone who has been stealing must steal no longer, but must work, doing something useful with their own hands, that they may have something to share with those in need.

Do not let any unwholesome talk come out of your mouths, but only what is helpful for building others up according to their needs, that it may benefit those who listen. And do not grieve the Holy Spirit of God, with whom you were sealed for the day of redemption.

Get rid of all bitterness, rage and anger, brawling and slander, along with every form of malice. Be kind and compassionate to one another, forgiving each other, just as in Christ God forgave you. Follow God's example, therefore, as dearly loved children and walk in the way of love, just as Christ loved us and gave himself up for us as a fragrant offering and sacrifice to God. **– Ephesians 4:26-5:2**

My dear brothers and sisters, take note of this: Everyone should be quick to listen, slow to speak and slow to become angry, because human anger does not produce the righteousness that God desires.

Therefore, get rid of all moral filth and the evil that is so prevalent and humbly accept the word planted in you, which can save you. Do not merely listen to the word, and so deceive yourselves. Do what it says. Anyone who listens to the word but does not do what it says is like someone who looks at his face in a mirror and, after looking at himself, goes away and immediately forgets what he looks like. But whoever looks intently into the perfect law that gives freedom, and continues in it – not forgetting what they have heard, but doing it – they will be blessed in what they do.

Those who consider themselves religious and yet do not keep a tight rein on their tongues deceive themselves, and their religion is worthless. Religion that God our Father accepts as pure and faultless is this: to look after orphans and widows in their distress and to keep oneself from being polluted by the world. **– James 1:19-27**

For additional help

If controlling anger has become a problem for you or someone you care for, it may be time to seek help. The American Psychological Association provides valuable information and practical guidelines for gaining and maintaining control over anger. A good place to start is the article *Controlling Anger – Before It Controls You.*[8]

Another excellent resource is the book *The Anger Habit: Proven Principles to Calm the Stormy Mind* by Carl Semmelroth, PhD and Donald E.P. Smith, PhD, Sourcebooks, Inc., Naperville, Illinois, Copyright © 2004

---

[8] The American Psychological Association (APA), 750 First Street, NE, Washington, DC 20002-4242, Telephone numbers: 800-374-2721 or 202-336-5500. Website: www.apa.org/topics/anger/control.aspx

Chapter 5

GRIEF

"No one ever told me that grief felt so like fear. I am not afraid, but the sensation is like being afraid. The same fluttering in the stomach, the same restlessness, the yawning. I keep on swallowing." – **C. S. Lewis,** *A Grief Observed*

"For he has not despised or scorned   the suffering of the afflicted one; he has not hidden his face from him but has listened to his cry for help."
– Psalm 22:24

Thirty years ago, when I was still learning the ropes of ministry, I found myself in the middle of something I was not equipped to handle. I was leading a Saturday afternoon committee meeting when I was suddenly called out and given terrible news. Three members of our congregation, two teenagers and their mother, had just been killed in an airplane crash. The only surviving family member was the husband and father, whom I will call Ron. The private jet belonging to Ron's company had plunged into a swamp on its approach to a Louisiana airport, killing all six of those on board: Ron's family, two friends, and Ron's colleague (and best friend), who was piloting the plane. Ron had planned to be on the flight but at the last minute had to stay behind to complete a business deal. He saw them off and promised to catch a commercial flight to meet up with them later in New Orleans. It was a rendezvous that never took place.

I was told that Ron had gone home to prepare for his flight to the scene of the accident. I jumped in my car and drove to the family's home. When I arrived, the house was dark and the front door ajar. With trepidation, I stepped inside and called Ron's name. No response. I made my way from room to room but found no one. Where was he? Then I heard sounds coming from the basement that made me shiver. Heavy, labored breathing. I slowly descended the stairs to the family room. I could see no one but noticed that the breathing was coming from behind a chair in a dark corner of the room. I walked over and carefully slid the chair aside. There was Ron in a fetal position on the floor, rocking back and forth and staring straight ahead. I felt utterly helpless.

What to do? I leaned down and whispered Ron's name. No response. He was in a daze from having just lost everything. I stood over him and prayed for guidance. Finally, I dropped to my hands and knees, crawled to Ron's side, and sat there in silence. For over two hours, we huddled together staring through our tears into the shadow of death and saying nothing. I may have wrapped an arm around Ron's shoulder, but I doubt I did even that. I just sat there beside my friend in his house of mourning.

The following day our pastoral team gathered to plan a triple funeral that we knew would be attended by an overflow crowd. It fell upon me to eulogize Ron's two children. I don't remember what I said at the memorial service, but I will never forget how I felt that day: cold, nervous, and inadequate. In the midst of feeling speechless, I had to speak to hundreds of mourners longing to hear words of comfort and hope. What assurance could I give with grief gripping my throat so tightly? Death creates a deep void that words can never fill.

Grief does not discriminate

Among the Scripture passages most often read at memorial services are these: Psalm 23, John 14, Romans 8, and Revelation 21. That final chapter of the Book of Revelation is the Apostle John's vision of a realm beyond human pain and earthly suffering, beyond the boundary of death itself. I've read those mysterious words hundreds of times to grieving people gathered in rooms reeking of flowers or standing beside open graves. I have officiated at the funerals of family members and close friends while being heartbroken myself. How badly I needed comfort and courage on those occasions! Anyone who has had to deal with suffering and death on a regular basis knows there are no professional exemptions from the agony of personal loss.

In his book *A Grief Observed*, C. S. Lewis wrote this after his wife had died from cancer:

> *No one ever told me that grief felt so like fear. I am not afraid, but the sensation is like being afraid. The same fluttering in the stomach, the same restlessness, the yawning. I keep on swallowing. At other times it feels like being mildly drunk, or concussed. There is a sort of invisible blanket between the world and me. I find it hard to take in what anyone says. Or perhaps, hard to want to take it in. It is so uninteresting. Yet I want the others to be about me. I dread the moments when the house is empty. If only they would talk to one another and not to me.[9]*

Lewis found that his beloved wife took a part of him with her when she died. That is what death does. It leaves behind victims with deep, hollow chasms in their souls. Grief also feels like being crushed by an overwhelming weight. In fact, the English word "grief" comes from an old French word meaning "heavy burden." It is the unbearable weight one feels after a loved one dies. But it's important to understand that there are other losses that are just as painful as losing someone to physical death.

Grief is about loss...*any* loss

When our first encounter with grief comes at an early age, we suddenly have to face the fact that we are not the center of the universe and the world doesn't cater to our childish needs. So begins our adjustment to the harsh realities of a life filled with hellos and goodbyes. Even in the most joyous events — such as weddings and graduation celebrations — we experience unexpected pangs of grief in having to adapt to leaving one stage of life and entering another. But the layers of grief don't end there. Aging athletes grieve the loss of their physical prowess.

---

[9] From *A Grief Observed*, by C. S. Lewis, Harper Collins Publishers, San Francisco, 1961, p. 15.

Parents grieve an empty nest. Aging singles grieve the death of their dreams of marriage and having a family. Those who get divorced grieve the death of an intimate relationship. The elderly grieve as their eyes grow dimmer, their hearing fades, and their physical health declines. Not only are these transitions tough, they can be devastating.

It's true that getting old isn't for wimps, but let's go one step further. *Life* isn't for wimps! Surviving the gauntlet of life is very, very difficult. No wonder the first thing a baby does after entering the world is scream and cry. Had we known before birth what life had in store for us, we might have refused to leave our mothers' wombs. Thankfully, God, in His wisdom, does not provide prenatal previews of what's ahead. As wonderful as life is—and it *is* filled with wonder—sooner or later we discover that life throws losses at us. And, oh, how they hurt!

Grief's assumptions and solutions

I've presented the problem, but what is the solution? There *must* be a solution. As it is with learning to handle any of life's challenges, the best place to start is Scripture. The Bible presents the realities of our existence with absolute candor and doesn't sugarcoat the pain and suffering we face throughout our lives. The insights I find in these ancient writings ring true and have been confirmed by my own experience. Listen to how these passages speak with the authority of a wise mentor:

> *"The Spirit of the Sovereign Lord...has anointed me to proclaim good news to the poor. He has sent me to bind up the brokenhearted, to proclaim freedom for the captives and release from darkness for the prisoners."* (Isaiah 61:1)

> *"When the perishable has been clothed with the imperishable, and the mortal with immortality, then the saying that is written will come true: 'Death has been swallowed up in victory.' 'Where, O death, is your victory? Where, O death, is your sting?'"* (1 Cor. 15:54-55)

"Praise be to the God and Father of our Lord Jesus Christ, the Father of compassion and the God of all comfort, who comforts us in all our troubles, so that we can comfort those in any trouble with the comfort we ourselves receive from God." (2 Cor. 1:3-4)

"Brothers and sisters, we do not want you to be uninformed about those who sleep in death, so that you do not grieve like the rest of mankind, who have no hope. For we believe that Jesus died and rose again, and so we believe that God will bring with Jesus those who have fallen asleep in him." (1 Thess. 4:13-14)

All these promises share the same three assumptions:

1) Every person will have to cope with grief in this life.

2) There is genuine consolation available for our grief.

3) The source of our consolation is Jesus Christ.

In the 1 Thessalonians passage above, Paul announces that believers need not *"grieve like the rest of mankind."* Why is this? Because believers in Christ's resurrection have one thing that others do not have: **HOPE**. Death is not the last chapter in the believer's book. We've found the way out of the darkness.

I've had the privilege of ministering to many as they approached death's door—not only believers but also agnostics and atheists. Seeing how doubters and unbelievers have handled the dying process has convinced me that the absence of hope is worse than death itself. Life is empty if our only purpose is to survive and perhaps indulge in the occasional pleasure, or, if we're lucky, reproduce and contribute to the gene pool before we die. If this is the best life can offer, no wonder so many escape into materialism, drugs and alcohol, hedonism, or even suicide. Those who believe they are stuck in a random, absurd existence will try anything to fill the void and numb the pain. The person whose life is without transcendent meaning is vulnerable to depression, and depression is a state of chronic grief that torments the mind and starves the soul. The only remedy is hope.

The other side of grief

The 21st chapter of the Book of Revelation is a treasure trove of hope. John lifts the veil between this life and the next to give us a glimpse of a world transformed. No more stress. No more violence or war. No climate crisis, cancer, or pollution. No endangered species or human corruption. No lying, hatred, cheating, or fear. Here is a preview of an existence where every cursed thing in our world—every threat to health and harmony— is eliminated. It will be a place of supreme hope and perfect peace.

In the second verse, the author describes a "New Jerusalem," free of strife and disparity, where all relationships are restored. The unholy principles of our present existence will be replaced by the rule of love and perfect justice. God will set right everything that humanity has done wrong. A new sheriff will be in charge, and he will be the Lord Himself. Revelation 21:3 says, *"Look! God's dwelling place is now among the people, and he will dwell with them. They will be his people, and God himself will be with them and be their God."* Now jump ahead to verses 5-8: *He who was seated on the throne said, "I am making everything new!" Then he said…"It is done. I am the Alpha and the Omega, the Beginning and the End. To the thirsty I will give water without cost from the spring of the water of life. Those who are victorious will inherit all this, and I will be their God and they will be my children."*

Get this. When this new day comes, the grief in our hearts will evaporate. This is great news for some, but not for all. Justice produces winners and losers, as explained in the verses that follow: *"But the cowardly, the unbelieving, the vile, the murderers, the sexually immoral, those who practice magic arts, the idolaters and all liars — they will be consigned to the fiery lake of burning sulfur. This is the second death."* This part of the passage is often avoided because it presents a troubling reality. The righteous will receive a second life, but those whom Christ pronounces unrighteous will suffer a second death, an eternal death. Just as heaven is forever, so is hell.

For those of us with faith in Jesus, this is astoundingly good news. We will be released from grief…and anger. What anger?

The anger that comes with thinking God has dealt us a bad hand. Even though He has done nothing of the kind, hurt produces blame, and God is the easiest target. Grief is the pain of loss, so those who grieve often blame God for taking something from them, and this makes them angry. We see this loss-grief-pain-anger sequence wherever there is trouble. When an expectant mother suffers a miscarriage. When a once beautiful marriage deteriorates. When an innocent child is abused. How can a loving God allow these things to happen? While losses in life are inevitable—and grieving over them is normal and healthy[10]—what if grief infects our spirit and turns us against God? Blame, anger, and resentment only compound our misery.

Revelation 21:4 goes a long way to comfort us in loss. John writes, *"He will wipe every tear from their eyes. There will be no more death' or mourning or crying or pain, for the old order of things has passed away."* God sees every tear we shed. He feels our pain and suffers with us. As long as this world endures—and until the new world arrives—our hearts will break and tears will flow. However...*HOWEVER*...it won't be like this forever! A time is coming when all death, all mourning, all pain, and all anger will pass away. It is God's sacred promise. Today we cry, but tomorrow our tears will dry.

In 1991, Conor Clapton, the four-year-old son of musician Eric Clapton, crawled out a window in his mother's Manhattan apartment building and fell 49 floors to his death. Afterward, from the depths of his grief, Clapton wrote *"Tears in Heaven"* as a lament over losing his son. The theology in the lyrics is spot on. *"Beyond the door, there's peace, I'm sure. And I know there'll be no more tears in heaven."* I know nothing about Mr. Clapton's beliefs, but his vision of the next world is consistent with the vision in the Book of Revelation. There are no tears in the realm of redemption where God gives His loved ones new life.

---

[10] In her book *On Death and Dying*, Elizabeth Kubler-Ross lists five stages of healthy grieving: Denial, Anger, Bargaining, Depression, and Acceptance. Link: http://psychcentral.com/lib/the-5-stages-of-loss-and-grief/000617

The grief-free zone

According to the New Testament's vision of heaven, as soon as we pass over the threshold of death, we leave behind the woes of earth. We won't hover above and watch surviving family members struggle through life. Scripture doesn't provide the details, but it appears that even if we are allowed some awareness of what's happening on earth after we die, we won't be grieved. After all, how could we observe from heaven the suffering of loved ones on earth and remain dispassionate? Wouldn't remaining emotionally attached to the pain we left behind disrupt our heavenly peace? Living in the eternal realm and the temporal realm simultaneously doesn't make sense. To me, it seems reasonable to assume we won't suffer the distress of this world once we enter the next. The details are a mystery to us, but I'm counting on being relieved of my worries, pains, and grief once I enter heaven.

My recent lesson on grief

One of my pleasures in studying the Bible is discovering something new each time I read it. This happened again as I studied John 14 in preparation for writing this chapter. Two thoughts arose that had not occurred to me earlier.

First, when Jesus prepares his apostles for the coming of the Holy Spirit during their final meal together, he gives the third member of The Trinity a name: Comforter (also translated Advocate, Helper, or Counselor). This is telling in that it foreshadows the troubles Jesus' friends will face following his departure, and it assures them that divine comfort (advocacy, help, or counsel) is at hand. The bad news is that they will need comfort; the good news is that God will provide it. Of the many names Jesus could have given the Holy Spirit—Defender, Teacher, Disciplinarian, Coach, Exhorter, or countless others—the defining label is Comforter. This speaks volumes to the millions who have suffered (and continue to suffer) grief until Christ returns to bring lasting peace.

Second, Jesus also assures his friends that they will never be alone in the midst of their troubles and grief. This is a powerful promise for a community riddled by death. When a loved one dies, the person may be gone but the relationship continues. My parents died many years ago, but my relationship with them remains intact. Of course, it has changed, but it's still there. I think of them, dream of them, imagine conversing with them from time to time. These are living relationships that survive after death. We grieve losing the people we love, but we continue to cherish and engage in our relationships with them. This is a game-changer that comes with faith in a God who transcends the material world.

These two revelations have strengthened my resolve, lifted my spirit, and expanded my vision. Perhaps they will do the same for you. As Jesus says in the last sentence of Matthew's gospel (Matt. 28:20), *"And surely I am with you always, to the very end of the age."*

Life after grief

In closing, I return to Ron's story. A couple years after losing his family, Ron attended a Bible class I was teaching. I opened the hour by inviting folks to greet those around them. Ron reached out and shook the hand of an attractive brunette sitting beside him, a single woman named Janet. Little did I know what would come of this handshake.

A few months later, I stood facing Ron and Janet in the very spot where, years before, I had eulogized Ron's deceased children. What was once a house of mourning had been transformed into a house of joy as we celebrated Ron and Janet's wedding. The shine of a new beginning erased the shadow of death. Years further on, Ron was the proud father of three new sons, and his grief had been replaced by gratitude.

I should tell you that Ron's "second life" has not been all hearts and flowers. He and his family have endured challenges and setbacks. Both Ron and Janet have survived bouts with cancer. Ron was nearly killed in a speedboat accident and has had other near misses. They have experienced illnesses, deaths, dramas, and traumas. No real-life story ends with "happily ever after;" that's the stuff of fairy tales. However, Ron's story bears witness to the power of faith and God's way of turning tragedy into triumph.

As I look back over the 40-plus years that I have known Ron and his two families, I see how the bad times strengthened our friendship as much, or more, than the good times. Ironically, the bitter tears have made those good times even sweeter. Sharing the full spectrum of life with Ron has connected us eternally. It's a beautiful mystery. When we enter into another person's grief, we discover that faith is the glue that repairs broken hearts and bonds souls together.

C. S. Lewis pondered divine grace and made this observation: *"Heaven will solve our problems, but not, I think, by showing us subtle reconciliations between all our apparently contradictory notions. The notions will all be knocked from under our feet. We shall see that there never really was any problem."*[11]

When life throws problems at us, we should remember that our problems are not problems for God. They may overwhelm us, but they never overwhelm God. Our present grief is painfully real, but it is not forever. Tears clear the eyes of faith to see what is prepared for us on the other side. We don't have to have all the answers if we trust in the One who does. Belief trumps grief.

Additional readings

The Spirit of the Sovereign Lord is on me, because the Lord has anointed me to proclaim good news to the poor. He has sent me to bind up the brokenhearted, to proclaim freedom for the captives and release from darkness for the prisoners, to proclaim the year of the Lord's favor and the day of vengeance of our God, to comfort all who mourn, and provide for those who grieve in Zion — to bestow on them a crown of beauty instead of ashes, the oil of joy instead of mourning, and a garment of praise instead of a spirit of despair.

---

[11] *A Grief Observed*, by C. S. Lewis, p. 83.

They will be called oaks of righteousness, a planting of the Lord for the display of his splendor. They will rebuild the ancient ruins and restore the places long devastated; they will renew the ruined cities that have been devastated for generations. **– Isaiah 61:1-4**

When the perishable has been clothed with the imperishable, and the mortal with immortality, then the saying that is written will come true: "Death has been swallowed up in victory." "Where, O death, is your victory? Where, O death, is your sting?" The sting of death is sin, and the power of sin is the law. But thanks be to God! He gives us the victory through our Lord Jesus Christ. **– 1 Corinthians 15:54-57**

Praise be to the God and Father of our Lord Jesus Christ, the Father of compassion and the God of all comfort, who comforts us in all our troubles, so that we can comfort those in any trouble with the comfort we ourselves receive from God. For just as we share abundantly in the sufferings of Christ, so also our comfort abounds through Christ. If we are distressed, it is for your comfort and salvation; if we are comforted, it is for your comfort, which produces in you patient endurance of the same sufferings we suffer. And our hope for you is firm, because we know that just as you share in our sufferings, so also you share in our comfort. **– 2 Corinthians 1:3-7**

Brothers and sisters, we do not want you to be uninformed about those who sleep in death, so that you do not grieve like the rest of mankind, who have no hope. For we believe that Jesus died and rose again, and so we believe that God will bring with Jesus those who have fallen asleep in him. **– 1 Thessalonians 4:13-14**

Chapter 6

REBELLION

"Every act of rebellion expresses a nostalgia for innocence and an appeal to the essence of being." – **Albert Camus, The Rebel: An Essay on Man in Revolt**

"I used rebellion as a way to hide out. We use criticism as a fake participation." – **Chuck Palahniuk, Choke**

I have a question for you. Did Jesus and his followers start a rebellion?

Before you answer, consider this definition: "Rebellion, uprising, or insurrection is a refusal of obedience or order. It may, therefore, be seen as encompassing a range of behaviors aimed at destroying or taking over the position of an established authority. Those who participate in rebellions...are known as 'rebels.'"[12]

Now, according to this definition, was Jesus a rebel? Many believe he was.

Rebellion as a rite of passage

When it comes to rebellion, what starts as an attempt to buck the system ends up becoming a system unto itself. As my generation entered our teens in the 1960s, we began to see ourselves as rebels and were proud of it. We thumbed our noses at social conventions by growing our hair long, dressing in bizarre clothes, imbibing various forbidden substances, playing loud music, and expressing a growing resentment toward those in authority. Along with many of my peers, I marched for peace and added my voice to the refrains of

---

[12] http://en.wikipedia.org/wiki/Rebellion

protest. "Make love, not war! Don't trust anyone over 30! Burn your draft cards! Burn your bras! Sex, drugs, and rock and roll, baby!"

But over the course of the next 30 years something happened. We who had been hippies morphed into yuppies (young urban, or upwardly mobile, professionals). Our idealism gave way to materialism. We turned our attention from peace-making to pleasure-seeking. Our counter-culture became a comfort-culture. As young people, we were determined not to sell out, so we dropped out, lashed out, and freaked out. Then we got older and all we wanted to do was *go out...*to expensive restaurants! Like every generation before us, we proved that "what goes around comes around."

Rebellion and religion

The repeating cycle of rebellion can also be seen in the history of the Church. When institutional religion turns stale, lifeless, and irrelevant, people discard traditionalism to break out on their own. They either reinvent the old faith or dispense with religion altogether. In recent years, we've seen this scenario unfold as charismatic preachers, trendy music, and state-of-the-art media shows are employed to revive faltering congregations. In one way or another, successive generations try to cover the cracked walls of long-established institutions by slathering on their own cultural preferences.

In 15th century Europe, the invention of the printing press increased public literacy, giving impetus to the Reformation and weakening Rome's stranglehold on Christendom. It's no coincidence that the root of the word Protestant is "protest." Martin Luther and his fellow reformers did not set out to ignite a socio-cultural rebellion, but that's exactly what they did. However, the story doesn't the end there. Those who originally tried to reform the Roman Catholic Church from within met such resistance that they were forced to break away. Within a few decades, these so-called "apostates" formed their own denominational structures, many of which became state churches. The cycle of rebellion was complete. So it goes with most counter-culture movements. What begins in heated dissatisfaction cools down and eventually hardens, forming new institutional comfort zones.

I entered the ministry at a time when many were abandoning the Church because it was "stale, boring, and irrelevant." Sound familiar? As young churchgoers, we didn't relate to the style of worship that our elders preferred, with its dirge-like hymns, pulpit platitudes, and redundant liturgies. How strange it was for me years later to find myself "running the show." Stranger yet, I'm now one of the old, institutional guys. But I still find myself grumbling about worship. Go figure. My current complaints are about the volume of the praise band, lyrics that are painfully repetitive, and too many "commercials" being flashed on the big screens. This all proves again that what's hot today will not be tomorrow. And so the cycle goes. No generation has a monopoly on rebellion. Not even my own.

The roots of rebellion

In case you haven't noticed, Christianity is not a new religion. Its Jewish origins go back over five thousand years to the Old Testament narratives, from Adam to Noah to Abraham to Moses to David to Jesus...and beyond. Neither human nature nor the dynamics of faith have changed down through the centuries, so there must be something at the core of Judeo-Christian culture that accounts for its survival in the midst of the shifting tides of time. What could that "something" be? And how has it held the Church together throughout each new cycle of rebels demanding novelty and change?

The life of the prophet Samuel bridged two eras of biblical history, from the period of Israel's territorial judges to the establishment of Israel as a unified kingdom. In contrast to our own era, Samuel lived at a time when people yearned for more order and less individualism. The Israelites dreamed of becoming like the surrounding nations, having an established government, their own king and army, a centralized religion, and defensible borders. While today we rail against "the establishment" and cling to our "right of individualism," the Israelites coveted the national stature and security that come with a strong military. After centuries of living under slavery and wandering in the wilderness as tribal nomads, they dreamed of stability. They were sick of stumbling along aimlessly on their own.

The Israelites finally approached Samuel and begged him to anoint a king to rule over them. But God instructed the prophet to tell them that they didn't know what they were asking for. If their demands were met, it would lead to their undoing. They were not to be like other nations, saddled with having to serve corrupt worldly masters. As usual, the Israelites didn't listen and continued to hound the prophet until they got what they wanted. And what they got was King Saul, a tall, handsome, commanding figure who appeared to be the one destined to deliver the goods, nation-status and glory. But just as God predicted, Saul's life soon began to unravel. He fell into a tailspin of paranoia and depression, culminating in suicide and nearly taking the whole nation down with him.

We would be wise to listen to Samuel's ancient warning in the midst of our own nationalistic impulses. But I fear that his words are again falling on deaf ears. A latent spirit of rebellion resides in every human heart and when it awakens it can infect all of society. This rebel within is an ambitious kingdom-builder fueled by selfish yearnings and shortsightedness. While the Israelites desired a superman to rule over them, our lust for self-rule is just as powerful. We long to occupy the throne in the Kingdom of Me, a realm where one supreme ruler makes the decisions and all opposition is suppressed.

Saul, the rebellious ruler

As Samuel's narrative unfolds, it appears that the shepherd boy David is fated to play the role of the rebel. He is immediately trusted and loved by King Saul, but quickly he becomes a threat. Saul's paranoia about his attendant-turned-hero produces a jealous and murderous rage, causing David to flee for his life. And it doesn't take long for David to gather his own small army. Many of the Israelites choose the daring, young giant-killer over their unstable, aging king. The plot thickens. David and his band of rebels roam the kingdom as outlaws, but the *real* rebel in the story is Saul. His insane narcissism leaves him alienated from his people and separated from God.

Saul's rebellious spirit is exposed in 1 Samuel 15, a discomforting text for modern readers. God speaks through his prophet Samuel and orders Saul to attack the Amalekites and

---

"totally destroy all that belongs to them." But Saul gets it only half right. He slaughters his enemies but spares their livestock. This offends God for two reasons: first, it openly defies the divine command, and second, it is an act of wanton greed. Saul wants the plunder for himself and hopes to appease God with token sacrifices.

In the wake of Saul's disobedience and selfishness, Samuel confronts the king. *"Does the Lord delight in burnt offerings and sacrifice as much as in obeying the Lord?"* The prophet knows the answer before he asks the question, as shown in the next verse: *"To obey is better than sacrifice, and to heed is better than the fat of rams. For rebellion is like the sin of divination, and arrogance like the evil of idolatry. Because you have rejected the word of the Lord, he has rejected you as king."* In other words, the prophet wants Saul to know that God will not be mocked by public displays of false devotion by those whose hearts turn inward. And so it is when anyone who is all-show-and-no-go tries to deal with God. The outcome is never good. In such cases, rebellion has its own reward, and that reward is anything but rewarding.

Biblical democracy and idolatry

As Westerners, we tend to assume that ours is the best form of government. "Liberty and democracy for all" is our motto. However, in ancient Israel, government and religion were not founded on democratic principles. Since its beginnings, Judaism has recognized only one supreme ruler. Yahweh. He is the *only* King. Other gods are powerless idols. Israelite religion did not adhere to the laws of majority rule, equal representation, or consensual voting. If God said it, the Jews were expected to do it. There was no room for rebellion. Such an ideology does not sit well with those who feel entitled to self-determination. This explains why many in our culture find religion to be stifling. We have a problem with authority. *All* authority! "No one is going to tell us what to do because we are free!"

Since the end of the Second World War, we in the West have become allergic to authority. We're suspicious of and cynical about those who rule us. We judge them according to our own standards and decide whether or not we will allow them to hold office. After all, don't they work for us? Saul had a similar obsession with autonomy, which prompted Samuel's rebuke of the king in 1 Samuel 15:23: *"For rebellion is like the sin of divination, and arrogance like the evil of idolatry. Because you have rejected the word of the Lord, he has rejected you as king."* On the Old Testament's list of sins, rebellion against God ranks as one of the worst, right beside the conjuring of demons and communing with the dead. It's as bad as it gets.

The seed of rebellion produces an insatiable desire for absolute autonomy, and as it grows it seeks to usurp divine authority. We have an assortment of labels for this lust for control: freedom, independence, individualism, self-expression, uniqueness, eccentricity, quirkiness, and other euphemisms. Spin it as you wish, the root is the same: pride. Pride is the soil in which all other sins thrive. But it's worse than that. Pride will go to any extreme to defend itself, even unto death. Saul took the tragic trail of pride that all other rebels follow. Yes, even unto death.

The consequences of rebellion

Let's return to 1 Samuel 15. After being stung by Samuel's rebuke, Saul pleads for mercy, asking the elderly prophet to advocate on his behalf before God. Obviously, he was hoping for a reprieve. This sounds like repentance, but is it really? Notice that neither Samuel nor God respond with offers of mercy. At first this seems strange, since mercy is what one would expect of a compassionate God. But divine forgiveness does not come cheap, and it certainly didn't in Saul's case. The king's stubborn arrogance made him more concerned about winning and saving face than about repenting for his sins. There's a difference between genuine remorse and regret over getting caught. When inner rebellion leaves no room for self-examination and repentance, our cries for mercy are insincere and empty. And when that happens, God doesn't turn His back on us; we turn our backs on Him.

The Samuel passage shows the unraveling that occurs when rebellion takes hold of the human heart. Israel's first king—the leader the people had demanded—falls into depravity, causing thousands to suffer. First, he loses his mind. Then he loses his friends and also his family. In the end, he loses his entire kingdom and takes his own life (1 Samuel 31). Thus ends Saul's tragic tale.

Early in my Christian walk, I struggled with passages like this. But I struggle no more. I've learned that while God may protect us from the condemnation we deserve, He doesn't necessarily protect us from the *consequences* we deserve. We see this in rebellion. It is costly. Regardless of whether rebellion shows itself in the mistreatment of others, the adoration of self, or the violation of God's creation, every rebellious act hurts someone and destroys something. This consequential principle accompanies divine law.

Our Creator has placed us in an environment designed to run according to absolute rules and principles, all of which are for our own well-being. When we break these rules and principles, we suffer the consequences. And without this consequential suffering, things would be far worse. When we rebel against God, we separate ourselves from His will and live smaller, less fulfilling lives and damage our relationships in the process. Rebellion exempts us from the many benefits of participating in God's kingdom, leaving us to fend for ourselves in our own miserable, little kingdoms.

Taming the will

Consider what these biblical sound bites have in common:

"If you are willing and obedient, you will eat the good things of the land; but if you resist and rebel, you will be devoured by the sword." For the mouth of the Lord has spoken. (Isaiah 1:19-20)

As obedient children, do not conform to the evil desires you had when you lived in ignorance. (1 Peter 1:14)

Submit yourselves for the Lord's sake to every human authority: whether to the emperor, as the supreme authority, or to governors, who are sent by him to punish those who do wrong and to commend those who do right. For it is God's will that by doing good you should silence the ignorant talk of foolish people. (1 Peter 2:13-15)

In the same way, you who are younger, submit yourselves to your elders. All of you, clothe yourselves with humility toward one another, because, "God opposes the proud but shows favor to the humble." Humble yourselves, therefore, under God's mighty hand, that he may lift you up in due time. (1 Peter 5:5-6)

These passages confirm that we don't have the luxury of picking and choosing which authorities we obey and which ones we won't. Instead, our primary obligation is to tame our own willfulness and try to avoid imposing our authoritarian judgments and value systems on others.

Consider this scenario. Let's say I know for a fact that our local police force is rife with corruption. Am I now free to disobey the law? Does a corrupt law enforcement system give me an excuse for running a red light or exceeding the speed limit? If I think such excuses will protect me, I'm in for a rude awakening. Once I'm caught, the judge who handles my case will not be impressed by my defense. I still will have to pay the penalty.

Here's another way to look at it. Are children justified in disobeying their parents once they discover that Mom and Dad are imperfect and make mistakes themselves? Or, as employees, are we permitted to do our job however we choose because we think we are smarter and more competent than our employer?

To my point, are we who follow Jesus Christ free to interpret and apply the Scriptures according to how they align with our own desires and self-interests? When the interpretation of any law—and the decision of whether or not to obey it—is left to the individual, the end result is chaos. And when such an attitude is applied to biblical law, individualism erupts into all-out spiritual rebellion. If we feel we are above the law, we will find ourselves under something far worse. Moral anarchy.

Rebellion as attitude

Those of us who are in the final season of life seem to share a litany of complaints about the generations following us:

- Didn't anyone teach these kids about respect?
- They have an attitude of entitlement and don't think they have to pay their dues.
- They want rewards they haven't earned and figure the world owes them something.
- No one can tell them what to do, so they don't listen to anyone.

- They don't respect authority...not parents, not teachers, not bosses, not police. They know it all and want it all. Right now!

It has been said that adolescence is the best substitute for a lifetime of experience. Having been young myself (many years ago), I have experienced the arrogance of youth and felt its hubris. And even though I share some of my fellow pensioners' opinions about today's youth, I've found that the dynamics of rebellion don't change much from one generation to the next. Selfishness and a yearning for autonomy are natural urges among the young, but they are by no means age-exclusive. We can never escape the temptations of the heart and don't want to submit to anyone. Regardless of our age, we don't want anything or anyone to cramp our style and deprive us of our precious freedom. However, what we *can* do is learn to suppress self-absorption, delay gratification, and attend to the needs of others. If our base urges go unchecked, they turn into frustration, which can then escalate into personal and public rebellion.

As I reflect on my past, I find myself wondering what my parents and their friends discussed so many years ago. I can only guess. They probably commiserated about their obstinate and disobedient kids, their silly fads, bad attitudes, and poor decision-making. I'm quite sure our parents were just as troubled by our rebellious attitudes as we are by the rebellion we see in our own children. These things don't change. Once again, we see that what goes around comes around.

Normal rebellion and abnormal obedience

Tensions and conflicts are inevitable in a world where generational cultures clash. This is normal. But submitting to authority goes against our selfish nature. The Bible teaches respect for authority, even when we don't like or agree with those in authority over us. Not only are we told to respect them, we're also told to *obey* them. This is God's will. If we ignore this call for submission and obedience, we evade God's correction and risk losing His protection. A rebellious disposition hardens the heart and disrupts relationships.

Learning spiritual obedience is like going through boot camp. It forces us to grow up and take responsibility. Why do military officers demand unflinching obedience from their troops? Because once the bullets start flying, second-guessing authority can result in lives—even wars—being lost. In this day of free-form religion and designer spirituality, what does it mean to submit to God? Are we to blindly obey God like a soldier obeys his commanding officer? These are difficult questions for those who have been culturally conditioned to break away from tradition and cut new trails. And if all roads lead to God and all lifestyles are acceptable, how can one be better than another? Conforming to ancient standards and traditions is anathema in our post-modern culture of individualism and tolerance. Authority has fallen out of style. We can't hear the Master's voice if we don't believe there is a Master.

Putting culture aside, how about you? Do *you* have a problem with authority? If you do, you probably don't get along with others. And, perhaps, you never have. Which means it's also likely that you don't get along with God. Jesus said it is impossible to serve two masters (Matthew 6:24). So which master has your allegiance? Or are you under the impression that you serve *no* master? If so, your inner rebel is calling the shots. Ironically, those whose master is self are the least free of all. They are enslaved to pride, and the only way out is to admit guilt, submit to God, and accept the consequences. Of course, submission to God comes with orders attached. We must change. This is bad news for the ego, but the gift that comes with submitting to divine orders is having order restored in our lives.

So, let's return to the questions we started with. Was Jesus a rebel? And did he start a rebellion? I believe he was anything but a rebel. He was the *liberator* of rebels! He didn't instigate a rebellion; he suppressed one. Jesus entered our world to bring us back to where we belong, into a healthy relationship with our heavenly Father. And, in doing so, he rescued us from the ravages of internal rebellion.

Herein is the paradox. If refusing to allow Christ to be our Master is the formula for disaster, then turning back to him in obedience is the "Declaration of Dependence" that sets us free. What a concept! Servitude that saves.

Additional readings

Then Saul said to Samuel, "I have sinned. I violated the Lord's command and your instructions. I was afraid of the men and so I gave in to them. Now I beg you, forgive my sin and come back with me, so that I may worship the Lord."

But Samuel said to him, "I will not go back with you. You have rejected the word of the Lord, and the Lord has rejected you as king over Israel!" **– 1 Samuel 15:24-26**

"Come now, let us settle the matter," says the Lord. "Though your sins are like scarlet, they shall be as white as snow; though they are red as crimson,   they shall be like wool. If you are willing and obedient, you will eat the good things of the land; but if you resist and rebel, you will be devoured by the sword." For the mouth of the Lord has spoken.
– Isaiah 1:18-20

So I tell you this, and insist on it in the Lord, that you must no longer live as the Gentiles do, in the futility of their thinking. They are darkened in their understanding and separated from the life of God because of the ignorance that is in them due to the hardening of their hearts. **– Ephesians 4:17-18**

Therefore, with minds that are alert and fully sober, set your hope on the grace to be brought to you when Jesus Christ is revealed at his coming. As obedient children, do not conform to the evil desires you had when you lived in ignorance. **– 1 Peter 1:13-14**

Chapter 7
INNER TURMOIL

"The final wisdom of life requires not the annulment of incongruity but the achievement of serenity within and above it." – **Reinhold Niebuhr**

"Incongruity is the mainspring of laughter." – **Max Beerbohm**

"Grace is the absence of everything that indicates pain or difficulty, hesitation or incongruity." – **William Hazlitt**

Years ago, the *Edinburgh Evening News* printed this rather unusual article[13]:

The world's funniest joke was unveiled by scientists today at the end of the largest study of humour [sic] ever undertaken. For the past year, people around the world have been invited to judge jokes on an internet site as well as contribute quips of their own. The LaughLab experiment conducted by psychologist Dr. Richard Wiseman, from the University of Hertfordshire, attracted more than 40,000 jokes and almost two million votes. And the joke which received the highest global rating—submitted by 31-year-old psychiatrist Gurpal Gosall from Manchester [England]—was:

"Two hunters are out in the woods when one of them collapses. He doesn't seem to be breathing, and his eyes are glazed.

"The other guy whips out his phone and calls the emergency services. He gasps: 'My friend is dead! What can I do?' The operator says: 'Calm down, I can help. First, let's make sure he's dead.'

"There is a silence, then a shot is heard. Back on the phone, the guy says: 'OK, now what?'"

---

[13] The *Edinburgh Evening News*, October 3, 2002:
http://news.scotsman.com/funniestjokes/The-worlds-funniest-joke.2366108.jp

The article went on to give the following explanation for why this joke works in all cultures and for all ages: *"We find jokes funny for lots of different reasons. They sometimes make us feel superior to others, reduce the emotional impact of anxiety-provoking situations or surprise us because of some kind of incongruity. The hunter's joke contained all three elements."*

You may or may not agree that the joke is funny, but it's worth noting the part incongruity plays in humor. *Webster's Dictionary* defines incongruity as "the inner conflict a person has when his beliefs don't match his actions."[14] In the joke, the man's decision to shoot his friend is in conflict with his desire to save his friend.

Unfortunately, not all incongruity is humorous. Having worked with men for decades, I find that one of the biggest issues they deal with is moral/spiritual incongruity. Men are troubled by the lack of consistency between their professed values and beliefs and how they are actually living. Their inner conflict is raging.

Spiritual incongruity as dissidence

Imagine that you are a pianist seated at a perfectly tuned piano. If you strike the right keys in the right sequence and rhythm, melodic music will flow. But if you flop your hand down randomly on the keyboard, the sound produced will be painfully discordant. Something similar happens when our lives fall into moral or spiritual incongruity. If we try to perform when our conscience is racked with inner dissidence, we experience the discordant feeling that we are not what we want to be. There is no harmony. We know all the right notes but keep hitting the wrong ones, leaving us disheartened for failing to live up to our highest standards.

This is a problem not limited to religious people; it's a personal shortcoming of many in our world. Everyone struggles with a degree of moral inconsistency at times, when our words and actions do not synchronize with our innermost beliefs. Because we are spiritually flawed, we are incapable of keeping our lives in tune. It was this realization that brought me to Christ as a university

---

[14] *Webster's Revised Unabridged Dictionary,* © 1996, 1998 MICRA, Inc.

student. I began to sense a widening gap between my convictions and my lifestyle, and it troubled me. I sensed opposing value systems battling within me, so I altered my personality and compromised my values in hopes of reducing the conflict. When I was with my parents, or others I wanted to please, I played the part of the good boy, conservative and obedient. When I was with my rock and roll band mates and fellow druggies, I became the wild man, scoffing at conventions and willing to try anything. And when I was with my sweet, Christian girlfriend, I morphed into the romantic poet, sensitive and thoughtful. So it went, depending on whom I wanted to impress. Like a chameleon, I adapted my behavior to blend into my surroundings, but in doing so I became a tangled mess of incongruity.

Inner demons

In Mark 5:1-20, Jesus confronts a naked, masochistic demoniac in a Gadarean cemetery. Jesus stands his ground and asks the raving lunatic to identify himself. The man answers, *"My name is Legion, for we are many."* It is a chilling response, and also quite revealing. Within this tormented soul was an army of entities that had taken control of his personality and torn it apart. He was no longer a whole person. But suddenly those demons found themselves face-to-face with the sanest and most formidable man who ever lived. No wonder they were agitated and afraid. Their oppressive reign was under threat.

When any of us seek to win the favor of everyone around us, we risk being occupied by divisive forces. And if we're not careful, we too can fall victim to the "Gadarean Demoniac Syndrome." We become so confused by the cacophony of voices within that we no longer hear the voice of God. Foreign "invaders" take up residence in our personality and slowly suppress our true identity. It's less dramatic than being possessed by a legion of demons but just as dangerous.

Our streets—even our churches—are teeming with Gadarean demoniacs these days, individuals so embattled in their psyche that they have lost their identity. This inner turmoil is killing us and killing our society. It is a virus that's infecting our marriages, our families, our friendships, our work relationships, and even our

Christian fellowship. The first sign that invaders are at our gate is a deep sense of restlessness, followed by spiritual confusion and a crisis of conscience. We know how we want our lives to be, but we can't seem to get there because of the tug-of-war within. This incongruity slowly erodes our integrity.

Economic incongruity

There also is a state of incongruity that can be seen in our economy. It's less about GNP (Gross National Product) and more about GMP (Gross Moral Product). My former country-of-residence, Switzerland, serves as an example of this phenomenon. The Swiss are known for being fiscally conservative and ethically sound. However, their reputation has been stained in recent years. Some of Switzerland's brightest and best have been caught behaving like teenagers on a weekend binge with their parents' credit cards. Some of the supposedly staid Swiss bankers—known as the "gnomes of Zurich"—have become riverboat gamblers, recklessly and illegally filling their coffers with fast bucks. As these renegade dealings have come to light, the Swiss public has been shocked and embarrassed by the incongruity. How could their trusted leaders be involved in systemic larceny? The answer is obvious. Greed!

Somewhere along the line, those running the Swiss financial institutions lost their moral bearings and abandoned their religious roots, roots established in the Protestant Reformation. And lest any of us become smug and start pointing fingers, we should remember that greed and corruption have run rampant among money managers throughout the Western World for centuries, especially here in the United States. Such reprehensible behavior is all the more shocking given our history of belief in a God who is both lawgiver and judge. These convictions are at the core of Judeo-Christian culture. History shows that when societies stray from their founding principles, they turn to lesser things and adopt other values to replace the cracked foundations on which their once-solid house was built.

As we examine other aspects of our society, we discover that other of our institutional charter values have dried up like shells on a beach, once vital but now hollow inside. Or to use another metaphor, our values are like the ring of residue in a bathtub after the water has been drained. We can tell that the tub was full at one time, but now the water is gone. So it is in Western culture. The residue of biblical faith remains on us, but the Spirit has departed, leaving the tub empty. We have a semblance of religion but no real faith. No spiritual vitality.

Our insatiable appetite for love and approval

Just as an empty stomach rumbles for nutrition, an empty soul calls out for God. I realize this isn't the most lyrical of images, but it illustrates how our God-given appetite craves satisfaction. In his day, Paul the Apostle saw the gap between people's deepest yearnings and their behavior and realized the incongruity it was producing. *"Do not let what you know is good be spoken of as evil,"* he says in Romans 14. His observation would have been just as true had he written, "Do not let your *evil* be spoken of as *good*." Aren't similar value reversals happening in our day? There is a widening gap between how we want to be perceived by others and how we behave. Paul continues, *"For the kingdom of God is not a matter of eating and drinking* [in other words, outward actions] *but of righteousness, peace, and joy in the Holy Spirit, because anyone who serves Christ in this way is pleasing to God and receives human approval. Let us therefore make every effort to do what leads to peace and to mutual edification."*

Many biblical texts warn that serving Christ is likely to bring derision, even persecution. As true as this is, Paul presents another aspect of Christian service that is just as important. He says, *"...anyone who serves Christ in this way is pleasing to God."* Clearly, God is pleased when we do good deeds, but there's more to it than that. Paul adds, *"...and [that person] receives human approval."* The person who serves Christ also pleases *others*. Wow! Have you heard that before? We tend to think that pleasing God means we will likely offend others, especially non-believers, so we've come to accept that living out our faith makes us unpopular. No wonder our lives are so incongruent. Losing favor with others frightens us. We've been taught that gaining God's approval means losing human approval. According to Romans 14, this is bad theology.

How did we fall into believing that having a healthy relationship with Christ may lead to unhealthy relationships with others? According to Scripture, the opposite is true. Godly living makes *everything* better. It makes for a better society. Better schools. Better marriages and families. Better laws. Better government. Better friendships. It even helps us to sleep better because, as the old saying goes, "a clear conscience is the best pillow." Godliness and congruity are compatible.

Incongruity and conscience

In John 14, Jesus says, *"Peace I leave with you; my peace I give you. I do not give to you as the world gives. Do not let your hearts be troubled and do not be afraid."* We frequently ask God for peace, but do we realize what we're asking for? What we *want* can be quite different from what we *need*. Most of us want things like a reduced stress load, escapes from conflict, relief for our pangs of conscience, and simple solutions for our complicated problems. We want to rid ourselves of the tension in daily affairs. But is this what God wants for us? If God's agenda does not match ours, it usually causes pangs of incongruity.

Take inner peace as an example. What does it mean to have inner peace? This is one of the most misunderstood aspects of faith. We mistake personal comfort for personal peace. What if inner turmoil is actually a truer measure of God's presence than inner tranquility? When I have inner turmoil, it's often because I have fallen out of tune with God's Spirit. Ironically, when that happens, my inner turmoil isn't a sign of God's *absence*; it's a sign of His *presence*. Those alarms in my conscience are God's way of letting me know that something is going on that doesn't align with His will for my life.

Consider the implications. This means that inner turmoil is a good thing when it heightens my self-awareness and reveals there is something wrong. This prompts me to restore the spiritual balance I have lost. Perhaps this is what Paul meant when he wrote, *"The peace of God, which transcends all understanding, will guard your hearts and your minds in Christ Jesus."* God's peace is something the human mind can't comprehend. We long for peace without pain and serenity without anxiety, but when it comes to God's peace—and here is the paradox—turmoil may come with it. When this happens, the discomfort we feel alerts us to inner discord. We feel rumblings of incongruity in our conscience, and that incongruity is the tuning fork that gets us back on pitch, ending the dissidence and restoring harmony with the Divine.

Walking with Christ without stepping on toes

Winning favor with God does not necessarily lead to losing favor with others. I've found that when we lead godly lives, we actually attract others. More often than not, it is *ungodly* living that eventually repulses others. Godly living involves focusing on the other person, and most people find that attractive. According to Romans 14, *"If your brother or sister is distressed because of what you eat, you are no longer acting in love."* If our behavior, positive or negative, doesn't match our professed beliefs, we make God look bad and confuse those around us. Those who walk in love don't step on people's toes.

As God's representatives on earth, how are we to interact with those around us? How can we sow peace rather than conflict? Remember that God's peace isn't only about finding peace with God; it's also about living in peace with one another. The peace described in Scripture is both horizontal and vertical. Paul's second letter to the Corinthian church ends this way: *"Finally, brothers and sisters, rejoice! Strive for full restoration, encourage one another, be of one mind, live in peace. And the God of love and peace will be with you."* Paul understood that being at peace is about more than getting a good night's sleep. It defines who we are and what we do when we're awake. How we treat others. How we spend our time and money. How we carry ourselves in private *and* in public. In the relational space we occupy, which is more important, *feeling* good or *being* good? Shouldn't we strive for both?

Look at Romans 14:19 again. *"Let us therefore make every effort to do what leads to peace and to mutual edification."* If I'm reading this correctly, there is a direct correlation between affirming others and having peace myself. They are mutually dependent, not mutually exclusive. The end result should be *mutual* edification. How I treat others will affect how I feel about myself just as much as how I feel about myself will determine how I treat others.

Conscience as a divine tool

As uncomfortable as incongruity makes us feel, there is something far worse, and that is *not* feeling the strain of incongruity. One of the marks of a sociopath or psychopath is the lack of conscience, feeling no shame and no remorse. We know some of these sociopaths and psychopaths by name. Caligula. Nero. Hitler. Stalin. Manson. Pol Pot. Jeffrey Dahmer. Saddam Hussein. But the majority of those with such a moral deficiency avoid detection and notoriety. They are among the relatively small percentage of the population (approximately 4%) who are incapable of self-examination and immune to feeling guilt. There is no sense of incongruity in a pathologically ill personality. This explains how they find it easy to habitually lie, steal, commit physical and verbal abuse, and even engage in such horrendous acts as rape and murder. It is a mental illness with symptoms that include moral bankruptcy, spiritual death, and social devastation, proving that the only thing worse than having a bad conscience is having no conscience at all.

Our Creator designed us to have an active conscience. In Romans 2, Paul describes the conscience as the law God imprints on every human heart. And this is confirmed in Jeremiah 31:33 and Hebrews 10:16: *"I will put my laws in their hearts, and I will write them on their minds."* Our conscience is God's gift, and it is also our best friend. It sounds an alarm when correction is needed.

If we want peace in life, we have to filter our thoughts and pay attention to the cries of the heart. Not only are we to listen to those cries but also examine our lives and stay in step with Jesus Christ. Being in tune with God's Word and will is never easy. It's a daily discipline. The mark of spiritual maturity is living in a way that reflects our godly aspirations and reflects the person of Christ. The theological word for this process is *sanctification*, which means being cleaned out and cleaned up spiritually. This allows us to become an instrument of God's peaceful and beautiful music. The more in tune with God we are, the more the noise of internal conflict fades away.

Additional readings

The mind governed by the flesh is death, but the mind governed by the Spirit is life and peace. **– Romans 8:6**

Therefore let us stop passing judgment on one another. Instead, make up your mind not to put any stumbling block or obstacle in the way of a brother or sister. I am convinced, being fully persuaded in the Lord Jesus, that nothing is unclean in itself. But if anyone regards something as unclean, then for that person it is unclean. If your brother or sister is distressed because of what you eat, you are no longer acting in love. Do not by your eating destroy someone for whom Christ died. Therefore do not let what you know is good be spoken of as evil. For the kingdom of God is not a matter of eating and drinking, but of righteousness, peace and joy in the Holy Spirit, because anyone who serves Christ in this way is pleasing to God and receives human approval. Let us therefore make every effort to do what leads to peace and to mutual edification. **– Romans 14:13-19**

Do not be anxious about anything, but in every situation, by prayer and petition, with thanksgiving, present your requests to God. And the peace of God, which transcends all understanding, will guard your hearts and your minds in Christ Jesus. **– Philippians 4:6-7**

Chapter 8
IMPATIENCE

"It is easier to find men who will volunteer to die, than to find those who are willing to endure pain with patience." – **Julius Caesar**

"Patience is bitter, but its fruit is sweet." – **Jean-Jacques Rousseau**

"We could never learn to be brave and patient if there were only joy in the world." – **Helen Keller**

"I am extraordinarily patient, provided I get my own way in the end."
– **Margaret Thatcher**

The photographer for a national magazine was assigned to take photos of a great forest fire. The smoke at ground level was too thick to get any good shots, so he frantically called his home office to hire a plane.

"It will be waiting for you at the airport," his editor assured him.

As soon as he got to the small rural airport, sure enough, a plane was warming up beside the runway. He jumped in with his equipment and screamed, "Let's go! Let's go! Let's go!"

The pilot taxied the plane into the wind, and soon they were in the air. "Fly over the north side of the fire," said the photographer, "and make three or four low-level passes."

"Why?" asked the pilot.

"Because I'm going to take pictures! I'm a photographer, and photographers take pictures!" shouted the passenger with exasperation.

After a long pause, the pilot said, "You mean you're *not* the flight instructor?"

There's a moral to this story. "Haste makes waste." I was an impetuous kid, so I heard this aphorism more than I care to admit. To say that patience has been my Achilles' heel is to insult Achilles. He had only one point of vulnerability; I have so many, and my impatience is easily exposed. I have been restless and easily frustrated for as long as I can remember. My late mother's words still ring in my ears: "Richard! Can't you just sit still?" For me, "wait" has always been a four-letter word.

Waiting as suffering

A biblical word for patience is "long-suffering." It is a term that captures how it feels to endure long periods of waiting with nothing happening. As I've admitted, I don't suffer well for very long, which is why I'm a lousy fisherman. Sitting still for hours waiting for a fish to bite? Are you kidding me? Impatience also accounts for my failure to teach my wife how to drive a car with a manual transmission, how to use a computer, and many other things. Being a good teacher requires patience, especially within a family. My impatience is even reflected in my sports preferences. I'll take football, basketball, and ice hockey over chess, cricket, and golf any day. In every area of my life, my addiction to speed and action is a symptom of my chronic impatience. As you might have guessed, I have written this chapter for myself, but if you can relate, climb aboard.

The Bible has much to say about patience. It is fourth on the Apostle Paul's list of fruits of the Spirit in Galatians 5:22-23, following love, joy, and peace. Our English word "patience" is taken from the Old French word *pacience*, meaning, "to endure suffering."[15] The Greek word most frequently used in the New Testament is *makrothumia,* which is a contraction of *makros* (long or big) and *thumia* (temper). It can be translated literally as "to possess a long fuse."

The Bible connects impatience to sinful anger. I'll have more to say about this later. In my case, anger isn't the main issue. It's more complicated than that. My problem is a critical spirit that causes me

---

[15] From the etymology website:
http://www.etymonline.com/index.php?search=patience&searchmode=none

to become exasperated when others don't fulfill my expectations. And disappointment and frustration are fruits of the tree of anger, not fruits of the Spirit. If we truly desire to be more like Christ—more filled with the Holy Spirit—then we had best be prepared to prune away our bad fruit to allow God's fruit to sprout and grow within us. The challenge is to prune impatience from our lives in order to make room for the sweeter fruit of patience. But this takes time, and our addictions to instant gratification and busyness have warped our perception of time. While the length of a day is a constant, the length of an attention span is subject to fluctuation.

Patience is especially elusive in our day because waiting is no longer seen as a virtue in a society addicted to instant gratification. In addition, when we are confronted by a daunting problem or unpleasant task, it's tempting to retreat, hide, or surrender. This can lead to avoidance or procrastination, which is really *false patience* grounded in fear. Some are quite adept at feigning serenity to cover their fear of making a mistake, but fearful procrastination is the opposite of waiting patiently in faith. However, spiritual stoicism is not to be confused with spiritual fruit. Being patient in Christ does not mean being passive or uninvolved. That's more like apathy. Genuine patience, Christlike patience, is trusting God enough to allow Him the time and space to reveal His will to us before we act impulsively or give up completely.

This doesn't mean all procrastination is bad. Only fear-based procrastination is fruitless. When we slow down and seek God's guidance before making a decision or taking action, our procrastination is justifiable. Think of it this way: godly patience is good procrastination.

The New Testament word *makrothumia* (long-suffering) has nothing to do with resignation. As believers, we are not instructed to bide our time by sitting back to wait for things to unfold before us. The Scriptural challenge is to exercise patience and self-control at all times and in all things in order to avoid the trap of impulsivity. Impulsion happens when we don't think things through, give in to our feelings, and either act on or become immobilized by our emotions. In either case, patience buys us the time to look before we leap or fold.

Patience in prison

Several years ago, a man named Dan came to our church to tell his story of spending nine weeks in an Iranian prison after being falsely accused of proselytizing and spying in a Muslim country. He described how his mood shifted from despair to resignation to deep depression during his incarceration. As the weeks rolled by, he started to see that he was right where God wanted him. He discovered a higher purpose in the midst of his persecution and became a spiritual opportunist rather than a victim of injustice. As he saw God providing opportunities to influence his Muslim guards, he devoted himself to building relationships and sharing his faith with them. To Dan's amazement, not only did his captors listen to his message, they received Christ with open hearts. Dan, the prisoner, became Dan, the spiritual liberator.

If God can perform such a miraculous turn of events through a man locked up in a Muslim prison, think of the miracles He might do through those of us who are captive to other things. Dan's long-suffering witness turned his tormentors into friends, even friends of Jesus. But it took time. A lot of time. And it required a lot of patience. Dan's patience resulted in a happy ending to a story that began in misery. God specializes in using captives to set captors free. It is something He has done countless times throughout history and continues to do today.

Learning to wait for something good

In Romans 8:22-25, Paul compares life in this world to a woman suffering through childbirth. Listen to his words: *"We know that the whole creation has been groaning as in the pains of childbirth right up to the present time. Not only so, but we ourselves, who have the firstfruits of the Spirit, groan inwardly as we wait eagerly for our adoption to sonship, the redemption of our bodies. For in this hope we were saved. But hope that is seen is no hope at all. Who hopes for what they already have? But if we hope for what we do not yet have, we wait for it patiently."*

For the person of faith, this present existence is a spiritual maternity ward in which the Holy Spirit works through our pain to deliver new life. Our "old person" is stripped away to make room for our "new person." However, Paul reminds us that this miraculous rebirth requires patient waiting. It doesn't happen overnight but, given enough time, it happens.

The Old Testament patriarch Moses learned about patience the hard way. He spent the first 40 years of his life as Pharaoh's adopted prince. Unlike his fellow Israelites, who were enslaved to a foreign ruler, Moses' captivity was to the same ruler, but his cage was gilded. After killing an Egyptian slave master, Moses had to flee for his life and spent the next 40 years in another kind of prison, as a fugitive in the desert of Sinai. Decades passed. Unbeknownst to Moses, God was preparing him to lead the Israelites out of Egypt. When that moment of leadership came, it led to 40 more years of Moses trying to get Egypt out of the Israelites, a task that took Moses to the edge of his patience.

Poor, old Moses! One hundred and twenty years spent on a mission of deliverance only to die without ever setting foot in the Promised Land. Talk about unrewarded patience! Centuries later, Paul the Apostle may well have had Moses in mind when he wrote: *"Who hopes for what they already have? But if we hope for what we do not yet have, we wait for it patiently."* Moses waited. Oh, how he waited! But we shouldn't assume he died without envisioning the reward for his patience. Moses' long-suffering led to the founding of a nation.

Growing in patience means growing up

Throughout my life, I have attended church nearly every Sunday. As I look back, I recall being a restless boy squirming in hard pews in stuffy sanctuaries where preachers droned on and on about things that seemed senseless. Week after week, month after month, year after year, I was forced to sit there in uncomfortable shoes, choking neckties, and stifling suits. How did I endure it as a kid? At best, it seemed like an utter waste of time, and, at worst, it felt like cruel and inhumane punishment. However, as the years rolled slowly by, I began to glimpse new meanings in the monotony. Gradually my restlessness subsided, and I saw there are things in life that can be enjoyed only when sitting still. The disdain I once felt for ancient hymns and droning organs was replaced by the comfort of familiarity. Those old stained-glass windows became prisms that bathed me in warm, soothing colors. The rote prayers became lyrical bridges between the mundane and holy. Over time, I even discovered nuggets of insight in those once monotonous sermons. More surprising yet, I began to savor the calm silence. Something miraculous happened within me. A God-given patience replaced my restlessness, renewed my senses, and gave me a newfound sensibility.

This transformation equipped me to handle obstacles that have tested my patience throughout my journey: years of academia, marriage and parenting, decades of work, multiple moves, and many other challenges. As I have passed through each of these gauntlets, I have learned to adapt to my circumstances and allow events to unfold at their own pace without me pushing and shoving. I have discovered how long it takes to build healthy friendships and working relationships, to establish a good reputation, to stay in shape physically and keep growing spiritually. These things have happened very, very slowly, and I have found no shortcuts. As the axiom goes, "anything worthwhile takes time." But where does that leave the person who refuses to take the time?

Boredom: the enemy of patience

Ideally, the pursuit of sensory and sensual stimulation starts to lose its luster as we discover that the thrills of life are often accompanied by the *ills* of life. Addiction to stimulation brings with it a desire to avoid silence. The distractions of our world have increased our fear of boredom. And boredom makes us morally and spiritually vulnerable. As the proverb warns, "Idle hands are the devil's workshop." Boredom *is* dangerous. The fallout it produces includes temptation, perversion, impulsivity, poor judgment, and, to put it bluntly, stupidity. Boredom also is fertile ground for drug, alcohol, and sex addiction, thrill-seeking, and other vices. When life bores us, we seek new stimulants, diversions, and adrenaline rushes, tempting us to take unnecessary risks, some of which are life-threatening. Here's how it works:

- Boredom lures us into experimentation, which leads to...
- Habitual behaviors that provide stimulation, which leads to...
- Addiction, where obsessive lusts seize control over us.

The popularity of extreme sports like the X-Games, base-jumping, cliff diving, freeform climbing, off-piste snowboarding and heli-skiing proves our insatiable craving for an adrenaline rush. There is a restlessness within the human soul that tempts us to flirt with danger. As each death-defying challenge is conquered, we ramp up the risk factors and reduce the margins of safety. Could it be that some fear boredom more than they cherish self-preservation?

During the summer of 2014, there were 36 wingsuit fatalities in the Swiss Alps. They were listed as "recreational deaths," a euphemism for senseless tragedies. And yet, this sport grows more popular every year. Why? I have to think that, at least in part, it is due to an aversion to tedium and fear of boredom. The extreme sports industry was birthed in our *extreme impatience.*

The late Swiss physician and author Paul Tournier offered an insightful analysis of humankind's lust for stimulation in his brilliant book *The Adventure of Living.*[16] Tournier saw our insatiable appetite for novelty and adventure as the motivating force behind many of our decisions and actions. I think he is right. Because of our fear of boredom, we're willing to suspend our common sense, our rationality, and even our morality. Why? To get another fix. This makes boredom a mortal threat.

Impatience and boredom produce a gnawing agitation that stifles the soul's yearning for peace. Our senses are so heavily assaulted by superficiality and stimulation that we have become vulnerable to the allure of instant gratification, which may be instant but is anything but gratifying. Is there room for patience in a society that refuses to slow down and sees the denial of pleasure as foolish? Our chronically impatient world is running at such a pace that those who hesitate are left in the dust to rust.

Patience, pride, and pacing

Impatience leads to impulsivity, but there is a better way. The world appears to be out of control, but God operates in another realm and at a different pace. His providence unfolds slowly, and if

---

[16] *The Adventure of Living* by Paul Tournier, Harper & Row Publishers, New York, New York, 1965.

we are not patient, we may miss out on what He is doing. Sound bites and strobe lights stimulate our senses, but God's wisdom is unveiled by other means and requires a longer stretch of time.

One of the most overlooked phrases in Scripture is "wait upon the Lord." This command is given repeatedly in various forms:

- *"Wait for the Lord; be strong and take heart and wait for the Lord."* (Psalm 27:14)
- *"Be still before the Lord and wait patiently for him; do not fret when people succeed in their ways, when they carry out their wicked schemes."* (Psalm 37:7)
- *"The end of a matter is better than its beginning, and patience is better than pride."* (Ecclesiastes 7:8)
- *"...those who hope [wait] in the Lord will renew their strength. They will soar on wings like eagles; they will run and not grow weary, they will walk and not be faint."* (Isaiah 40:31)

These verses, and others like them, make the same point. Trust in God and remain patient. But also know that patience is elusive to those who are proud in spirit. Patience and pride, like oil and water, do not mix.

Reflect on the Scripture readings I've attached at the end of this chapter and consider the correlation between impatience and anger (see Chapter 4). Impatient people are not peaceful people. They are perpetually agitated, frustrated, exasperated, and quick to anger. Many truisms confirm this. "Patience is something we admire in the driver behind us, but not in the driver ahead of us."[17] As an old proverb says, "Patience is a virtue; possess it if you can, seldom found in woman, never found in man." Or, as Harvard professor Barbara Johnson puts it, "Patience is the ability to idle your motor when you feel like stripping your gears."[18]

---

[17] Adapted from a quote by Bill McGlashen, Executive Vice President of the Arizona AFL-CIO, Phoenix, AZ

[18] Barbara Johnson (b. 1947) is an American literary critic and translator. She is currently a Professor of English and Comparative Literature and the Frederic Wertham Professor of Law and Psychiatry in Society at Harvard University.

In a way, an idling motor is a helpful metaphor for understanding what it means to "live in Christ." An engine that has been idling is warmed up and ready to go at a moment's notice, even though the vehicle itself has remained still for a long time. Similarly, those who live in the Spirit (of Christ) are always ready to go but do not rush ahead. That disposition requires patience. Those who are spiritually alive never stop firing on all cylinders...even when sitting still.

Being still

Psalm 46:10 says, *"Be still, and know that I am God."* When was the last time you sat still long enough to feel—actually feel—the presence of God? I've seen people so revved up on the Spirit, so emotionally high, that they know only one speed: all out. But when it comes to resting in the Lord, they struggle. We are much more useful to God when we slow down and wait rather than spinning our wheels and burning out the clutch. Slowing down is hard enough, but for many of us, sitting still for long periods of time seems impossible. But it is not.

The Book of Ecclesiastes was written by a Jewish sage in his final season of life. That sage may have been King Solomon himself. In chapter 7, verse 8, he writes, *"The end of a matter is better than its beginning."* This is lost on the young, but as we age we start to get it. There comes a time when the end of something becomes more joyful and fulfilling than its beginning.

Do you recall how it felt to graduate and receive a diploma? Have you experienced the fulfillment of doing a job well and seeing it through to completion? Can you imagine what it's like to be a cancer patient who has just heard that her blood tests are clean and no more chemotherapy is necessary? Have you experienced the elation of making the final payment on a 30-year mortgage? All these things prove that *"the end is better than the beginning."* Eventually, everything in this world will come to an end, and that's not a bad thing. The tough part is waiting peacefully for that good ending to come.

The author of Hebrews gives an insight into life from God's perspective. In Hebrews 12:1, he writes, *"...since we are surrounded* by such a great cloud of witnesses, let us throw off everything that hinders and the sin that so easily entangles. And let us run with perseverance the race marked out for us." The meaning becomes even clearer if we substitute the word "patience" for "perseverance" here. "Let us run **with patience** the race marked out for us." There are races, and there are races. Some races are run with the goal of being the first to cross the finish line. Other races bring out the best in every runner regardless of his or her order of finish. The race of faith is the latter kind. We don't run to defeat others; we run to experience Christ's victory over sin and self. Faith is about being the *finest*, not the *fastest*. And creating anything fine requires time, perseverance, and, yes, patience.

Patience as a last resort

I wanted to wrap this up with some practical suggestions for how to become more patient. But as I thought about it, I realized this is silly. Patience isn't a formula to be applied or a lesson to be learned. One way to acquire patience is either by willingly letting go of our desire for control or by having that control taken from us. This happens only after we have exhausted our resources or come up against someone (or something) we cannot overcome. Then all we can do is wait.

We cannot "mount up on eagle's wings," as Isaiah says, so long as we are flying on our own power. God doesn't need high-fliers. He comes to the aid of those who have run out of fuel and sputtered to a stop. Patience is something that comes to individuals who are at the end of their rope. Patience is one of God's rewards to those who "hang in there." Once we let go of our need to control, God enters our waiting room and attends to us. This is another one of those paradoxes of faith. When there is nothing more we can do, God does *everything*. His Spirit enters the space we clear out for Him and fills the time we give Him.

Now, what are *you* waiting for?

Additional readings

I remain confident of this: I will see the goodness of the Lord in the land of the living. Wait for the Lord; be strong and take heart and wait for the Lord. **– Psalm 27:13-14**

Commit your way to the Lord; trust in him and he will do this: He will make your righteous reward shine like the dawn, your vindication like the noonday sun. Be still before the Lord and wait patiently for him; do not fret when people succeed in their ways, when they carry out their wicked schemes. Refrain from anger and turn from wrath; do not fret – it leads only to evil. For those who are evil will be destroyed, but those who hope in the Lord will inherit the land.

– Psalm 37:5-9

The end of a matter is better than its beginning, and patience is better than pride. Do not be quickly provoked in your spirit, for anger resides in the lap of fools. **– Ecclesiastes 7:8-9**

But the fruit of the Spirit is love, joy, peace, forbearance [patience], kindness, goodness, faithfulness… **– Galatians 5:22**

So do not throw away your confidence; it will be richly rewarded. You need to persevere so that when you have done the will of God, you will receive what he has promised. For, "In just a little while, he who is coming will come and will not delay." **– Hebrews 10:35-37**

Chapter 9
ILLNESS

"Illness is the night side of life, a more onerous citizenship. Everyone who is born holds dual citizenship, in the kingdom of the well and in the kingdom of the sick. Although we all prefer to use the good passport, sooner or later each of us is obliged, at least for a spell, to identify ourselves as citizens of that other place."
— Susan Sontag, Illness as Metaphor

"Each patient carries his own doctor inside him."
— Norman Cousins, Anatomy of an Illness

"A righteous man may have many troubles, but the Lord delivers him from them all." — **Psalms 34:19**

I've been blessed with health and vitality for most of my life, a blessing I have never taken for granted. During my first 55 years of life, I didn't spend a single night in a hospital bed. Of course, I have experienced my share of the usual aches, pains, and accidents that come with growing up, but these amounted to nothing worse than the occasional cut, bruise, broken bone, or childhood disease. However, in my late 50s, all of that changed. And how!

Oh no, there's something seriously wrong here

Sometime in 2006, I started to experience some fogginess in my head, accompanied by dizziness, disorientation, a sense of anxiety, and mild depression. I finally turned to my doctor for help. He found nothing abnormal and sent me to several specialists, each of whom poked, prodded, and scanned me from top to bottom. None of their examinations produced an answer. Throughout this ordeal, I continued my usual pace at work without anyone noticing that something was wrong.

119

As I look back now, I honestly don't know how I kept functioning. I continued to lead the church, preach, teach, counsel, write, make pastoral calls, and do everything else without slowing down or taking a break. As I shuffled from one doctor to the next, I clung to the hope that the right diagnosis would eventually come. But it didn't, and my symptoms only got worse.

Eventually I could no longer hide my desperation, so I sat down with a trusted friend and confessed my despair. He pledged to get me the help I needed and managed to book me into the Mayo Clinic in Rochester, Minnesota. If this famous health center couldn't get to the core of my problems, no one could. Susan and I flew to the States with high hopes of discovering once and for all what was affecting my health. Little did we know what drama and trauma was ahead of us.

My first appointment at "The Mayo" was with the physician who would manage my case. He listened to my story, checked me over, and sent me straight to radiology for a cranial scan (MRI). Within an hour, we received a call to return to the doctor's office immediately. I knew this couldn't be good. The doctor sat us down in front of a screen filled with images of my cranium and pointed to a dark shadow on the rear-left side of my brain.

"Mr. Davis," he said in a somber tone, "we don't know what caused this, but you have had a brain hemorrhage sometime within the last six or nine months."

I stopped breathing. An icy wave of fear swept over me. Susan and I stared at each other in stunned silence. After regaining some composure, I swallowed hard and asked in a shaky voice, "How serious is this, Doctor? Is it life-threatening?"

"Any cranial hemorrhage is serious," he explained, "and in your case, we can't be sure what's going on. But I can assure you that you're in the best of hands. We'll do everything in our power to get you the help you need."

Oh dear. I felt like a tragic melodrama was unfolding around me. For the next three weeks, I ran the full gauntlet of The Mayo's systematic examinations.

The plot thickened with each exam. My doctor had said, "Whatever is wrong with you, we'll find it. And, believe me, we *all* have *something* wrong with us." I knew he was trying to assure me that they would be thorough and diligent, but this did nothing to relieve my anxiety. My one consolation was that I knew I was in the hands of the world's best medical professionals. Surely, they could heal me.

As with many things in life, pondering the nature of something is far different than experiencing that "something" first hand. Philosophical reflection stops when fear and suffering appear. During my time at The Mayo, I had to face the possibility that I may not have a long and healthy life ahead of me. My illusions of longevity evaporated as I became aware of my vulnerability. Mortality was my new reality, and I never would be the same.

The Mayo maze...and the miracle

Our month at the Mayo Clinic was the hardest trial Susan and I had ever faced. I was the patient, but Susan bore the burden of watching and worrying as I endured the battery of tests. She spent hours in waiting rooms praying that the tests would come back negative and lead to something positive. Unfortunately, the worst was yet to come.

As I was completing the lengthy examination, my cardiologist recommended I have one more test. An angiogram. In his opinion, it wasn't necessary, but since we had traveled all the way from Europe, he deemed it wise. We reluctantly agreed. I was assured that it was a routine procedure with less than a one percent chance of anything going wrong.

I was given a mild sedative but remained conscious as the medical team inserted a long, narrow tube into an artery in my groin. The surgeon focused on a screen as he guided the device through my heart, into my vertebral artery up to the base of my skull. He then injected a stream of dye into the blood vessels of my brain. At that moment, the "less than one percent chance" happened. Somehow the pressurized stream of dye severed my vertebral artery, causing a hemorrhage inside my spinal vertebrae, a place where bleeding can't be stopped.

I looked into the masked faces above me and saw panic in their eyes. Alarms went off and more white coats swooped into the room. I was quickly wheeled off to the Intensive Care Unit, where I was hooked up to intravenous drips and electronic monitors. Situation critical! For the next 24 hours, not even my wife was allowed in to see me. She was told that something had gone wrong and my prognosis was uncertain.

It wasn't until later that we discovered the severity of my predicament, but Susan knew it was bad, so she jumped on her smartphone to alert our loved ones and ask for prayer. Our social network sprang into action. Family, friends, churches—even people we had never met—started to pray for me. I am still humbled today as I reflect on the wave of compassion that enveloped me during those crucial hours. I am certain that God heard and responded to those prayers because the bleeding inside my spinal column suddenly stopped. God intervened to help me beat the odds and recover from a potentially lethal accident. My healing was miraculous. Thankfully, God transcends statistical possibilities.

Early the next morning a team of doctors gathered beside my bed and tried to account for what had happened. They couldn't. They were baffled—although obviously relieved—that the crisis had passed. The fact was, I had suffered a brain hemorrhage and a dissected vertebral artery and lived to tell about it. More amazing yet, I continued to function more or less normally throughout both ordeals. I was able to resume my full work schedule within two months.

So, was this a miracle? I should add that I had already experienced two other inexplicable healings earlier in my life: a torn ACL that mysteriously reattached itself and a broken bone in my foot that mended overnight. This is why belief in divine miracles isn't a stretch for me. I have experienced God's healing power first hand on several occasions, so I am convinced that He performs miracles today just as He always has. For me, this isn't a problem. But I still grapple with other perplexing questions about divine intervention. For example, why do miracles happen for some and not for others? And how, when, and where do they happen? Do they require certain conditions, and what role does faith play in these miracles? Even though I accept that there may not be answers to these questions, I can't stop wondering.

Why me?

I often wonder why I survived my brush with death that day in the ICU while others in that same hospital going through their own life-and-death struggles did not. I have no answer, other than having to acknowledge that God is free to do whatever He chooses…as well as whenever, wherever, and with whomever He chooses. I've learned that our speculations about these things are usually fraught with bad assumptions, warped theology, and, above all, ignorance. We simply do not have the information or wisdom to understand these mysteries. And if we were given such revelations, we don't possess the brainpower to process them. In the end, perhaps we're better off accepting God's sovereignty rather than constantly trying to figure Him out.

Within circles of faith, many controversies surround our debates about the nature of human illness and the reality of divine intervention. One of our hottest questions is whether or not God heals *every* person who sincerely asks for His healing. Some say, "Yes, He most certainly does, so long as the person asks in faith." They cite biblical accounts of Jesus healing the many who came to him. While this may demonstrate a simple (and commendable) faith, I think it often reveals a *simplistic* faith. And there is a big difference between simple and simplistic.

It is never wise to draw sweeping conclusions from a few disconnected biblical verses. When we do this, we run the risk of squeezing God into our own little, doctrinal boxes. If God heals *every* sick person who calls out to Him in faith, what are we to do with the many healings that *do not* occur in the Bible? For example, in 2 Corinthians 12:7-10, Paul the Apostle admits to suffering from a "thorn in [his] flesh" and admits to having asked God on at least three occasions to remove it. As far as we know, that healing never came.

However, in this passage we see that Paul had come to realize something about his affliction. He saw that his suffering was a protection from conceit in that it caused him to rely more heavily on God's all-sufficient grace. He discovered that his shortcomings exposed inner needs that only God could fill. Rather than seeing these things as handicaps, Paul came to accept that his limitations expanded his spiritual capacity, allowing the Spirit to equip him to work more effectively for God's kingdom. The more Paul leaned on God, the more God propped him up.

Personal testimonies often focus on our weaknesses and God's power to fix whatever is broken, which can leave us feeling like beggars pleading for God's mercy. No wonder many find these testimonies off-putting. It's a bitter pill to swallow for those who take pride in their autonomy and self-reliance. Paul's confession reminds us that self-reliance is a form of idolatry. When we fight God for control of our lives, God always wins. Sooner or later we exhaust our human resources and come up short. How will we ever accept help if we never admit that we need it? And this applies to our physical health just as it does to every aspect of lives. Thankfully, there are times when God refuses to fix what is broken in order to grow our reliance on His strength rather than our own. As I said, it's a bitter pill. But bitter pills can produce sweet results.

If God is for us, why do we hedge our bets?

Here is a practical question. If God is capable of healing every illness, why invest in health insurance or seek medical care?

Surprisingly, Scripture is loaded with references to the essential role that physical medicine plays in our lives. The New Testament author Luke was a physician by profession. (He is often called "Dr. Luke.") There is no reason to think his doctoring stopped once he became an evangelist or that his faith in God's healing power made his medical training obsolete. Scripture says nothing to suggest that belief in God and the practice of medicine are anything but complementary. After all, isn't the goal of both "professions" — the profession of faith and the medical profession — to make people healthy and whole?

If faith healing is meant to replace medical healing, as some suggest, why did Paul instruct the young pastor Timothy (in 1 Timothy 5:23) to *"stop drinking only water, and use a little wine because of [his] stomach and [his] frequent illnesses"*? Why didn't Paul instruct the church leaders to heal Timothy by laying hands on him? We know that Paul exercised the spiritual gift of healing a number of times by applying physical touch (see Acts 19:11-12). He even brought a dead man back to life with an embrace in Acts 20:7-12. And yet, in 2 Timothy 4:20, we are told that Paul left Miletus without healing a sick friend named Trophimus. If Paul had the gift of healing and could dispense it freely, why did he apply it in some cases but not others? Apparently, the nature of healing is a bit more complicated than we think.

There is abundant biblical proof that health maintenance is a cooperative effort between God and humanity. The Old Testament is full of references to the positive role medicine plays in our world.[19] Entire sections of Exodus, Leviticus, Deuteronomy, and other books are devoted to giving practical advice for food preparation, personal hygiene, and the prevention and treatment of diseases. These guidelines were given to the Israelites while they were under the special care of the Almighty. Why would such guidelines be necessary if God was on duty to attend to their health?

---

[19] 2 Kings 20:1-11; Job 13:4; Isaiah 1:6; Jeremiah 8:22; 30:12-13; 46:11; and Ezekiel 27:17

It seems that even God's chosen ones were expected to be responsible for maintaining their own health. For all of us, preventing sickness requires sensibility and healthy habits.

The New Testament adds more illumination to the subject. In Matthew 10:1-8, Jesus empowers his disciples to heal the sick and injured on his behalf. We also see this in Jesus' parable about a compassionate Samaritan who gives medical aid to an injured man along the road and then enlists an innkeeper to help (in Luke 10:25-37). The lesson being that we are responsible for caring for one another. Further on, in Luke 17:11-19, Jesus heals ten lepers and sends them to the local priest to be examined because community health was the responsibility of religious leaders in ancient Israel. It's also interesting that in Luke 5:31, Jesus says, "People who are well do not need a doctor, but only those who are sick." He is stating the obvious: sick people actually do need doctors and should rely on them. Yes, miracles happen, but more often than not, God doesn't circumvent the existing health care systems to do His healing. He works with and through them.

Trust in God...and pass the medication

Obviously, not all medical professionals consciously partner with God as they make their rounds. Doctors and nurses are only human. As with any profession, there are good ones and bad ones. None of us should exercise blind faith when seeking healing. We must choose our caregivers carefully and entrust our bodies only to those who have integrity and a record of competency. Be skeptical of those who ignore, discredit, or reject traditional medicine in order to push their own agenda. And be especially wary of anyone who tells you that religious activities alone (prayer, meditation, sacrificial giving, etc.) are enough to bring about healing. Such claims are reprehensible and shouldn't be trusted.

My own experience in providing care for others—and receiving it myself—has convinced me that cooperating with medical professionals is the way to go.

It is naïve to rely <u>only</u> on faith healers. If we believe that God is indeed the source of all healing, how does consulting a competent physician violate that conviction? God is behind *all* healing irrespective of the agent or method through which it comes. Whether the healing comes by means of the natural or supernatural, to God be the glory!

It's not all about me

I think it's important to add that I've seen medical professionals come to faith in Christ as a result of having witnessed "miraculous" healings in their own faith-filled patients. We should remember that healing may come to those who *provide* the care as well as to those who *receive* it. It's been said that the measure of any society is how its weakest members are treated. If this is true, it makes sense that God's Spirit would use our own suffering to minister to the wider circle of those who are suffering around us. Not only does God minister to the one who is ill, He uses the illness as an opportunity to strengthen and grow faith in others. The patient is not the only one that the Great Physician attends to. When we are in the worst of health, God brings out the best in those who care for us. This is a silver lining on the cloud of suffering that is often missed.

Being ill within God's will

When it comes to faith and health, the lingering question behind all other questions is: why do we get sick in the first place? If God loves us and wants us to be healthy and whole, what has gone wrong? According to the Book of Genesis, pain, suffering, death, and the other troubles of life are consequences of our spiritual rebellion. Romans 8:18-22 states that all of creation is currently "frustrated" and "groaning" in pain as a result of humanity's fall from grace. All of these texts communicate the same message: when we choose *our* own way over *God's* way, we lose paradise.

Until Christ returns to restore our paradise-lost, we have to deal with the mess we've made of things. We can't blame God for the troubles we've brought (and continue to bring) upon ourselves. Illness is not God's doing, it's the result of what *we've done* to the world He gave us.

One of God's greatest gifts to us is free will, but we have abused that gift. Like our original ancestors Adam and Eve, we have chosen to become free agents, and that has opened the floodgate of bad decision-making. That's the bad news. But here is the good news. In the next world, we will be given "eternal eyes" to see that most, if not all, our earthly travails are the result of our willful and selfish pursuits, both individually and corporately. These travails are not divine curses. Once we get our new eyes, we will realize how we've knocked the natural balance out of whack. This is as true in our inner world as it is in our outer world. We have corrupted our environment and our own health just as we have corrupted every other aspect of God's design. Why has God allowed this? Why doesn't He simply step in and make right what we have made so wrong?

Consider this. If God took it upon Himself to correct all our mistakes, where would He start? And where would He stop? Imagine the Creator of the universe trailing along after us cleaning up every big and little mess we make. In a scenario like this, one would have to wonder who really has control. If God devoted Himself to distributing remedies for every human misery, miracles would no longer be miraculous. They would become commonplace out of necessity. When the supernatural becomes commonplace, the natural order is disrupted, and God's set boundaries are violated. We do not live in a universe where the Creator serves the created. Even if God fixed the many things we break, what would keep us from breaking them again? Our chronic brokenness is a symptom of something deeper. We have heart disease.

The devil, you say

Another layer of this discussion is the question of the role evil plays in sickness. I am suggesting it is *less* than we think...and also *more* than we think. Satan is the personification of evil in Scripture, so we must come to terms with his involvement in our suffering.

The Bible never states that all illness is the result of demonic activity. On the contrary, there are many places in Scripture where sickness and disease are treated as normal conditions in life. Based on the gospel record, Jesus' direct confrontations with demonic activity and demon possession were rare. The forces of evil are not even mentioned in the majority of miracle accounts. This is not to say that evil plays no part in our health, but it does suggest that evil is not the predominant factor. This is why we should be cautious when drawing conclusions about the causes of (and remedies for) our infirmities. If anyone tells you that all physical and mental illnesses are evidence of demonic activity, be very careful. While evil spirits have been known to harass believers on exceptional occasions, *demons cannot possess a believer*. If they could, the primary function of medical providers would be spiritual deliverance rather than physical care.

A Comment on the Demonic

The Bible does not state explicitly whether a Christian can be possessed by a demon. However, since the Holy Spirit dwells within believers (see Romans 8:9-11; 1 Corinthians 3:16; 6:19), doesn't it seem unlikely that God would allow demons to co-exist within the hearts of those He has claimed as His own? While we recognize this is a controversial issue, mainstream Christianity holds to the belief that a true believer cannot be possessed by a demon. There is a difference between being possessed by a demon and being oppressed/influenced by a demon.

Demonic possession involves an evil entity occupying our being in order to control our thoughts and/or actions (i.e., Luke 4:33-35; 8:27-33; Matthew 17:14-18). Demonic oppression is different. This involves a demon or demons attacking a person spiritually and trying to entice or influence him/her into sinful behavior (1 Peter 5:8-9; James 4:7).

In the New Testament passages that deal with spiritual warfare, we are never told to cast a demon out of a believer (Ephesians 6:10-18). We are to resist the devil (1 Peter 5:8-9; James 4:7) rather than cast him out. (Explanation adapted from: gotQuestions?org: http://www.gotquestions.org/Christian-demon-possessed.html)

Given the breadth and depth of this topic, I will not go into it further here, but I do recommend that you do some study on your own. There are many excellent resources available to guide you. I do believe there are times when demonic activity contributes to (or even causes) illness, but such instances are exceptional. However, the effects of evil are far more common than post-modernists and materialists would have us believe. This explains my "more and less" comment earlier.

I am convinced that on those rare occasions when demonic activity (or demon possession) occurs, God is fully able to exert His power to deliver and heal the afflicted. We should not give the devil more credit than he deserves. The Old Testament story of Job serves as a reminder that God limits the devil's ability to attack believers. It isn't a contest of equal powers.

Faith healers and fake healers

There is another question I want to address. What are we to make of faith healing and faith healers? Again, we must be very cautious. Nowhere in Scripture do we see the Holy Spirit empowering someone to exercise the gift of healing indiscriminately, on a whim, or for selfish reasons. No one has God's healing power on tap to dispense whenever, or to whomever, he or she chooses.

God doesn't create superheroes with superpowers. The God of the Bible distributes His gifts according to His will, not according to our will. Paul speaks of this in 1 Corinthians 12, where he explains the nature of the spiritual gifts. Never do *all* God's children receive the same gift. And never does one person get all the gifts. Nor can any of us exercise our particular gifts all the time.

God alone controls the flow of spiritual gifts. If that is true — and I believe it is — we should be very skeptical of those who bill themselves as "faith healers," especially if they use their "gift" for personal gain. When the Holy Spirit bestows any gift, it is for the glory of God, the building-up of His kingdom, and to benefit His people. Beware the itinerant healer who comes to town as a showman! God doesn't put on shows; He grows souls.

Divine intervention by divine prevention

God wants us to know how to prevent illness. This is why He gives laws and decrees, dietary and health codes, rules of social and governmental order, and relational guidelines. The Bible puts far more emphasis on *prevention* than on healing. As parents, we do everything possible to keep our children from getting sick or injured, right? We would never intentionally expose our children to health-threatening risks. So why would a loving God do such a thing to His children? Is He less caring and protective of His children than we are of ours?

God is perfectly — yes, *perfectly* — aware of the dangers we face in this fallen world. Thus, He watches over us with a high level of attention and affection. He doesn't zap us with germs and diseases. He is not the instigator of accidents and disasters. In fact, if we make an honest assessment of our troubles, I think we can see that most of our troubles are self-created. Think about it. How many of our problems are the result of our own (or someone else's) selfishness or disobedience? Most of the hazards we face are of our own making. Someday — perhaps in the next world — this will be revealed to us.

Until that time, the best way to stay healthy is to live a healthy lifestyle. Likewise, the best way to stay close to God is to live a *godly* lifestyle. That's how life works, and it isn't complicated. If we live recklessly, sooner or later we will have a wreck. And when that happens, we shouldn't expect God to be our personal paramedic. We live in a world where our habits and poor judgments eventually catch up with us.

When we ignore the Rule-maker and become a rule-breaker, we make a mockery of the protective provisions God has provided for us. We reduce His abundant grace to a few "pills" to be pulled out and swallowed whenever we're hurting. But there are no such magic pills. Staying healthy in mind, body, and spirit is a lifestyle. And the Great Healer is more about preventative medicine than prescription medications.

Health starts with obedience. We obey God's laws out of gratitude for His protection, not to gain it. Why expect the Lord to work miracles on our behalf when He has already provided the greater miracle of inviting us to live in an ongoing relationship with Him here and now? Placing our lives in God's hands will not protect us from life's troubles, but it does change how we handle those setbacks and find the strength to rise above them. Living in Christ doesn't mean never getting sick; it means maintaining spiritual health in the midst of sickness.

Additional readings

Jesus went through all the towns and villages, teaching in their synagogues, proclaiming the good news of the kingdom and healing every disease and sickness. When he saw the crowds, he had compassion on them, because they were harassed and helpless, like sheep without a shepherd. Then he said to his disciples, "The harvest is plentiful but the workers are few. Ask the Lord of the harvest, therefore, to send out workers into his harvest field." **— Matthew 9:35-38**

He went down with them and stood on a level place. A large crowd of his disciples was there and a great number of people from all over Judea, from Jerusalem, and from the coastal region around Tyre and Sidon, who had come to hear him and to be healed of their diseases. Those troubled by impure spirits were cured, and the people all tried to touch him, because power was coming from him and healing them all.
— **Luke 6:17-19**

Praise the Lord, my soul; all my inmost being, praise his holy name. Praise the Lord, my soul, and forget not all his benefits – who forgives all your sin and heals all your diseases.... — **Psalm 103:1-3**

He sent forth his word and healed them, and rescued them from the grave. — **Psalm 107:20**

My son, pay attention to what I say; turn your ear to my words. Do not let them out of your sight, keep them within your heart; for they are life to those who find them and health to one's whole body.
— **Proverbs 4:20-22**

Surely he took up our pain and bore our suffering, yet we considered him punished by God, stricken by him, and afflicted. But he was pierced for our transgressions, he was crushed for our iniquities; the punishment that brought us peace was on him, and by his wounds we are healed. We all, like sheep, have gone astray, each of us has turned to our own way; and the Lord has laid on him the iniquity of us all. — **Isaiah 53:4-6**

Heal me, O Lord, and I will be healed; save me and I will be saved; for you are the one I praise. — **Jeremiah 17:14**

He said to them, "Go into all the world and preach the gospel to all creation. Whoever believes and is baptized will be saved, but whoever does not believe will be condemned. And these signs will accompany those who believe:

In my name they will drive out demons; they will speak in new tongues; they will pick up snakes with their hands; and when they drink deadly poison, it will not hurt them at all; they will place their hands on sick people, and they will get well." — **Mark 16:15-18**

Is anyone among you sick? Let them call the elders of the church to pray over them and anoint them with oil in the name of the Lord. And the prayer offered in faith will make the sick person well; the Lord will raise them up. If they have sinned, they will be forgiven.

— James 5:14-15

Chapter 10
TEMPTATION

"There is always free cheese in a mouse trap." **– H.C. Diefenbach**

"No man knows how bad he is till he's tried very hard to be good." **– C.S. Lewis**

"Lead me not into temptation; I can find the way myself." **– Rita Mae Brown**

The Christian tradition of giving up something worldly during Lent has its origins in practices that predate the birth of Christ. For centuries devout men and women of every faith have committed themselves to a lifestyle of asceticism, denying the pleasures of the flesh in hopes of establishing a more intimate connection with God. This self-denial may include celibacy, restrictive diets, abstaining from alcohol, and avoiding sensual stimulation. Ascetics strive to avoid what tempts them most in order to demonstrate to God, others, and self how serious they are about their spiritual aspirations. These practices continue today both within and without religious circles—from candidates for the priesthood to athletes in training—because delaying (and denying) gratification is seen as proof of devotion.

Depending on our background, many of us have adopted a particular set of assumptions about how God views our engagement with the things of this world. The more religious we become, the more likely it is that we will feel pangs of self-consciousness and guilt about our material comforts and sensual urges. For many Christians, godliness and worldliness don't mix. They envision the Almighty as a strict taskmaster, or angry policeman, who reprimands those who fall into the clutches of carnality. Such believers are easily intimidated by temptations of any kind, even if these so-called temptations are merely passing thoughts or natural desires.

Desire vs. temptation

Not every desirous thought is a temptation. From the moment of birth, we start dreaming about things we long to experience or possess, but most of our dreams dissipate without leading us into immorality. Temptation happens when desire takes root in our psyche and causes preoccupation with a lustful urge. Once we become convinced that satisfaction and contentment will come *only* by giving in to that urge, the obsession begins. Giving in to temptation compromises our higher nature (God-given conscience) and leaves us at risk of becoming enslaved to lust. This is how it tends to play out. First, we have the thought. Then we "entertain" that thought by giving it more and more mental space. So begins our journey down the road of temptation. As soon as we act upon that tempting thought, we fall into sin. If that sin is engaged in repeatedly, a sinful habit is formed. And habitual sinning can lead to addiction. What began as an idle thought quickly spirals into moral and spiritual degeneration that may be inescapable.

Regardless of how strong we think we are, we must never underestimate the power of temptation because it creates an insatiable longing to indulge in things that our Creator forbids. It's no coincidence that the Bible's first moral lesson is called "the first temptation." The same serpent that tempted Adam and Eve in the Garden of Eden comes to tempt us all, exhorting us to indulge our appetites, seize control of our own lives, and, ultimately, turn against God. This begins the war.

We may say we want to please God, but we can't resist giving in to our own desires. When Jesus said it is impossible to serve two masters (Matthew 6:24 and Luke 16:13), he was speaking of the temptations that come with the struggle between our higher and lower natures. This is the oldest and fiercest battle every person fights. It was Adam and Eve's first crisis, and they lost! You know the story. But how many of us know that there will be a *last* temptation? It is foretold in Revelation 20:7-15. At the end of history, Satan will make one final, desperate attempt to separate us from God. However, the outcome of the last temptation will be very different from the first. It will not succeed. And the tempter, the devil, will be cast into "the eternal fire." At that time, God will restore creation by re-establishing what was destroyed at the beginning. This is our great hope. What started in temptation will end in triumph.

Unfortunately, until the final act is played out, we remain caught in the tension between the first and last temptations and continue to suffer the consequences of the first couple's failure. Since we have yet to receive the full release secured for us in Christ's death, we fight to survive in a world that is spinning away from God and assailing us with volleys of temptation.

Of the many Scriptures I could cite on this topic, one of the best is Psalm 119:1-11, which teaches that personal discipline is our first defense against temptation. In these verses we find the psalmist's formula for peace and happiness. This formula is in direct opposition to the worldly formula for happiness. If you desire real peace, here's how to attain it. Lead a blameless life. Live in a way that is so in tune with biblical teaching that no one would dare accuse you of wrongdoing. Seek after God in everything you do. Follow His rules. Guard your mind and soul, and don't let them stray. Do these things and you will be a happy camper. More than that, you will never again have to take a sleeping pill. As has been said, "the best remedy for insomnia is a clear conscience."

Loving the fight

I believe that one reason we struggle unsuccessfully against temptation is because we actually *enjoy* the struggle. It turns us on. If we're honest, don't we relish our temptations? They titillate and energize us. We salivate at the thought of getting a taste of forbidden fruit. In The Lord's Prayer, we ask God to "lead us not into temptation," but do we really want His protection? Think about it. Does God actually lead us into temptation? If so, the Bible contradicts itself. James 1:13 proclaims that *"no one, when tempted, should say, 'I am being tempted by God'; for God cannot be tempted by evil and he himself tempts no one."* Jesus tells us to ask God not to lead us into temptation. But James says that God never tempts anyone. So which is it? We need to sort this out.

At first glance, reconciling The Lord's Prayer with James' statement appears to be linguistically challenging. But let's dig deeper. The biblical languages have seven words to describe testing and tempting. In English, we generally use only the two words "test" and "tempt." Greek is even more precise. The Lord's Prayer appears twice in the gospels, first in Matthew 6:9-13 and again in Luke 11:2-4. In both passages, the same word is translated "temptation." Later, in the first chapter of James (verses 2-3 and 12-14), that same Greek word is used seven times, being translated as "trial" twice and as "tempt" the other five times. In these three short passages, the *same* Greek word is translated "trial" four times and "temptation" five times. Because the translators used different words, how can we know the real meaning? Such word-parsing may bore you, but stay alert and read on. These words matter.

Single words with many meanings

As is always the case when studying the Scriptures, we must consider how each word is used within a particular context and how it is used throughout the entire document. Misunderstandings occur when we lift words and verses out of their contextual flow. For example, look at how we use the English words "trial" and "test." Try to make sense of the following paragraph:

> "Before I go to **trial** today, my patience will be **tested** by having to go through a **trial** run of my chemistry **test**. After that, I begin a **trial** period of **testing** my new car with time **trials** at the track. That's why I'm a bit **testy** at the moment."

Here the same two words have eight different meanings, and each can be understood only by looking at the context. This is part of comprehending any language, but it's especially important when it comes to examining words we believe are divinely inspired. Such is the case when trying to understand how the New Testament uses the words "tempt" and "test."

If we ask God to protect us from temptation, shouldn't we expect Him to do so? And if He doesn't, are we left to make our own way through a minefield of temptations? Not a chance! A righteous God never sets us up to fail. Which means that even temptation is somehow used by God for our betterment. Scripture warns that blaming God for our moral failings is bad theology. In fact, it is *dangerous* theology.

God doesn't play with our emotions to see how far He can push us before we break. What kind of parent would do that to a child? Good parents know that testing is a part of childrearing. But it's impossible to shield our children from all temptation, so we try to give our kids the tools and strength to resist temptation on their own. Isn't this what we ask of God regarding temptation? As human parents, we don't set temptation traps for our children, so why would the perfect Parent do this? There's a difference between testing children and tempting them. We know that. And we also know that God is infinitely wiser than we are in handling His children, especially when it comes to reducing risk and providing reward.

Testing vs. tempting

During our time in Belfast, we lived in the downstairs flat of a house owned and occupied by my brother-in-law and his family. It fell upon me to drive our two kids and their three cousins to and from school every day. As was my habit, I kept coins to pay for parking in a compartment between the two front seats in my car. One day I noticed that the coins were disappearing faster than I was using them. I became suspicious and wondered if one of my kids...or one of my nephews...had been stealing them. I hoped I was wrong, but I had to know, so I set a trap.

One day before picking up the kids after school, I refreshed the coin supply and recorded the amount. After returning home, I quickly opened the driver's door, jumped out and ran in the house to a window where I could watch the kids get out. They quickly dispersed. All but one nephew. He remained in the backseat until the others were gone. Then he looked in all directions, opened the compartment where I kept the money, and snatched a handful coins. Oh, no! My nephew was a thief, and I had caught him red-handed.

Next came the hard part. I had to figure out how to handle the situation without humiliating the boy or damaging family relationships. I waited for the right moment to confront my nephew. As expected, he was embarrassed and ashamed and quickly admitted his guilt. I asked him what he thought we should do about it. To his credit, he offered to pay whatever he had stolen and within days did so. That nephew is now grown up and has six children of his own. I couldn't be prouder of the man of integrity he has become. The one-time thief is now a fine father and leader in his church. Beautiful.

Here's my question. Did I *tempt* my nephew, or did I *test* him? At the time, I considered several options for resolving the issue. I could have stopped leaving coins in the car. But what would that have accomplished? Removing the temptation may have ended the thievery, but what would it have done for the thief? Imagine what might have happened had I not caught my sneaky nephew in the act. Who knows? He may have moved on to more sophisticated crimes, with higher stakes and more severe consequences. What if his deception and larceny became habitual? What if law enforcement had to step in later to do what the lad's uncle should have done earlier? That story would have had an unhappier ending.

As I've spent many years studying God's parenting, I have come to recognize and appreciate His ways. I am convinced that God has placed us in this world of tension and temptation not to *break* us...but to *make* us. He does not tempt us with evil, for that violates His very nature. But He certainly tests us. And tests us. And tests us again, over and over. I believe He doesn't do this to give us a chance to prove ourselves to Him but rather to provide us with opportunities to prove *to ourselves* that we are capable of rising above this fallen world and overcoming our fallen nature. With God's help, we learn to resist temptation and, thus, gain spiritual confidence and develop godly character. Aren't these the divine test results we all hope to receive?

Being at our best by taking the test

How can I know if I'm good at math if I've never taken a math test? The same could be asked about any competency I think I've achieved. I can't know anything about my capabilities unless they have been tested. Even when it comes to my faith, how can I know I am devoted to God if my devotion has never been put to the test? How can I trust an untested faith to sustain me during times of failure, regret, disappointment, grief, and suffering? The fact is, I can't. Until I have been tested.

I've learned a few lessons as I've journeyed down the rocky road of temptation. Failure is a powerful teacher. First of all, I no longer ask God merely to steer me away from temptation. I've taken that prayer one step further. I now ask God to keep me far away from any situation in which temptation might arise. If I get too close to certain things, I know I can't trust myself. One doesn't play with fire in a house full of kindling. Not only do I ask God to protect me from potential danger, I plan my steps to align with that prayer.

With so many temptations readily available, I've learned to live defensively. That's why sources of sexual temptation are off limits for me, just as they should be for anyone committed to marital fidelity. That's why, as a pastor, I have never handled the church's money. That's why I don't have secret dealings with people, hang out alone in bars, or engage in gambling. That's why I have a qualified person do my taxes and allow other trusted friends to have access to my computers and financial records. That's why I have mentors and accountability partners. I have put these safeguards in place to reduce my chances of falling into temptation. And this isn't because I don't trust God; it's because I don't trust *myself.* I am convinced that trusting too little in God isn't what sets me up for failure. Failure comes with trusting too much in myself.

The temptation trap

The late Howard Hendricks was a leading voice in the American church. Years ago, Hendricks interviewed 246 men in full-time ministry who had lost their positions because of sexual immorality.[20] His survey found **four factors** that all those men shared:

1. None of them was involved in any kind of personal accountability group with other men.
2. Every one of them had ceased to have a daily time of personal prayer, Scripture reading, and worship.
3. Over 80% of them became sexually involved with women they were counseling. (In other words, they were spending significant amounts of time in private, intimate conversations with women other than their wives.)

---

[20] *Finishing Strong*, by Steve Farrar, Multnomah Books, Sisters, Oregon, 1995, pp. 29-30.

4. And finally, without exception, every one of those 246 men was confident that moral failure "will never happen to me."

I don't know if a similar survey has been taken of women who have succumbed to sexual temptation, but I suspect the factors would be largely the same. Proverbs 16:18 says, *"Pride goes before destruction, a haughty spirit before a fall."* How true, how true! Pride kills because it brings with it the illusion of autonomy and invulnerability, and this has nothing to do with gender. Both sexes are prone to getting caught in the web of pride, and temptation is the point of entrance. Once we're caught, there's no easy way out.

The subtlety of temptation

Temptation happens when we fall for the devil's promises of pleasure and comfort, when all he really has for us is pain and suffering. Temptation is the bait, but pride is the trap. The devil is the master deceiver whose biggest lies start with the whisper, "You can handle it." By the time we discover that we *can't* handle it, it's too late.

I want to make an important distinction here. I don't think our deepest struggles are with the obvious temptations; I think they are with the subtler ones. The sins that do the most damage are not sins of the flesh but sins of the heart. There's no question that sexual lust, alcohol, drugs, materialism, gluttony, and other such obvious cravings do great damage. But the truly lethal temptations are the ones we don't realize are there. And even if we do recognize them, we often refuse to diffuse them. These are the temptations that smolder deep within us, day after day and year after year. Unless the temptation is exposed and confessed, it's impossible to defeat it and move on. As long as the temptation is ignored or denied, it will have its way with us.

As I said, the greatest temptations are not necessarily the obvious ones. Some of us are tempted by the need always to be right. This is so subtle, but so damaging. It pushes us to defend our rightness so vehemently that we attack, even destroy, anyone who threatens our delusion of superiority. This is the sin of *unconfessed temptation* that hides behind a smokescreen of pride.

I've known people who believe they're so spiritually and morally superior that they can't tolerate the "imperfect" people around them. They secretly hold them in contempt. Jesus saves his harshest words for those who pretend to have all the answers but never question themselves. Jesus warns us to watch out for them. They have succumbed to a temptation that hardens the heart and fortifies a kingdom of self-rule. Their contempt for others makes contentment with God impossible. Temptation thrives behind their ramparts of self-righteousness.

Looking forward to giving in to temptation

Make no mistake. We can fool ourselves, but we can't fool God. How can we ask God to keep us away from temptation while willingly indulging in the very things that weaken us? How can we expect God to protect us from the sins that we secretly plan in our hearts even as we pray? Unholy intentions can't be hidden from the One who looks into our darkest corners. If we honestly want God to clean our spiritual house, we can't keep the doors locked.

In summary, we need to remember that temptation is not a sin. It is simply a fact of life. Jesus himself was tempted. However—and this is a big however—Jesus never gave in to temptation. Sinning only happens once we surrender to temptation. As risky as temptation is, and as hard as it pulls at us, we need to realize that there is nothing wrong in feeling tempted. Feeling guilt about thoughts we can't control but have never acted on produces *false guilt*. The guilt is not real. Allowing others to exercise undue influence over us is a set-up for false guilt. The same is true of entertaining and believing the devil's lies. I repeat, thoughts come and go. Test each new thought to discover its source before you buy into it. Allowing those thoughts to influence our actions expands the gap between us and others, and between us and our Maker.

Today we're told that there is no such thing as sin. That it's merely a mental construct. Scripture says otherwise. The Bible tells us to flee from sin (1 Tim. 6:10-11), from sexual immorality (1 Cor. 6:18), from idolatry (1 Cor. 10:14), from the evil desires of youth (2 Tim. 2:22). When we do this, we are not the only ones taking flight. James 4:7 makes this promise: *"Resist the devil, and he will flee from you."* As we resist temptation and obey God, the tempter flees from us. We don't have to chase him. If we stand our ground, he will turn tail and run, taking his temptations with him.

We are not the ones most vulnerable in this battle against temptation. The devil is. If he loses, his realm is weakened. We have the Holy Spirit watching over us, but our enemy doesn't. The devil wants to make us allies, but the alliance can't happen without our cooperation. The devil's crew is an army of willing volunteers, and temptation is one of his primary recruiting tools. Thankfully, we can refuse to allow that tool to be used on us. Temptation's only power is the power we give it. At the moment we resist temptation, God Almighty moves in, and the devil flees in fear.

One of the most assuring words on temptation comes from the famous 23ʳᵈ Psalm: *"Even though I walk through the darkest valley, I fear no evil [or temptation], for you are with me."* While we can't avoid life's dark valleys, as God's children, we never pass through them alone. Giving in to temptation causes isolation, but resisting temptation brings us deeper into God's circle of companionship and protection. That's the safest place.

Additional readings

Blessed are those whose ways are blameless,   who walk according to the law of the Lord. Blessed are those who keep his statutes   and seek him with all their heart — they do no wrong   but follow his ways. You have laid down precepts   that are to be fully obeyed. Oh, that my ways were steadfast   in obeying your decrees! Then I would not be put to shame   when I consider all your commands. I will praise you with an upright heart   as I learn your righteous laws. I will obey your decrees;   do not utterly forsake me. How can a young person stay on the path of purity?   By living according to your word. I seek you with all my heart;   do not let me stray from your commands. I have hidden your word in my heart   that I might not sin against you.

— **Psalm 119:1-11**

144

We should not test Christ, as some of them did — and were killed by snakes. And do not grumble, as some of them did — and were killed by the destroying angel. These things happened to them as examples and were written down as warnings for us, on whom the culmination of the ages has come. So, if you think you are standing firm, be careful that you don't fall! No temptation has overtaken you except what is common to mankind. And God is faithful; he will not let you be tempted beyond what you can bear. But when you are tempted he will also provide a way out so that you can endure it. **— 1 Corinthians 10:9-13**

Therefore, since we have a great high priest who has ascended into heaven, Jesus the Son of God, let us hold firmly to the faith we profess. For we do not have a high priest who is unable to empathize with our weaknesses, but we have one who has been tempted in every way, just as we are—yet he did not sin. Let us then approach God's throne of grace with confidence, so that we may receive mercy and find grace to help us in our time of need. **— Hebrews 4:14-16**

Consider it pure joy, my brothers and sisters, whenever you face trials of many kinds, because you know that the testing of your faith produces perseverance. ... Blessed is the one who perseveres under trial because, having stood the test, that person will receive the crown of life that the Lord has promised to those who love him. When tempted, no one should say, "God is tempting me." For God cannot be tempted by evil, nor does he tempt anyone; but each person is tempted when they are dragged away by their own evil desire and enticed.
— James 1:2-3, 12-14

Be alert and of sober mind. Your enemy the devil prowls around like a roaring lion looking for someone to devour. Resist him, standing firm in the faith, because you know that the family of believers throughout the world is undergoing the same kind of sufferings.
— 1 Peter 5:8-9

Chapter 11
MARITAL PROBLEMS

"My wife has lived with at least five different men since we were wed — and each of the five has been me." — **Lewis Smedes**

"Men marry women with the hope they will never change. Women marry men with the hope they will change. Invariably they are both disappointed." — **Albert Einstein**

"Long marriages have ended in ruin over tiny and insignificant grievances that were never properly aired and instead grew into a brittle barnacle of hatred. — **Augusten Burroughs**

"Let the wife make the husband glad to come home, and let him make her sorry to see him leave." — **Martin Luther**

"It's more important to be the right person than to find the right person." — **Dr. Shirley P. Glass**

I grew up during a time when community clubs were a part of American life. Most of those were clubs segregated by gender. The men's clubs had names like the Lion's Club, Rotary International, the VFW (Veterans of Foreign Wars), the Kiwanis, the American Legion, and the Moose Lodge. Among the women's clubs were the PEO (Philanthropic Educational Organization), the PTA (Parent Teacher Association), the DAR (Daughters of the American Revolution), and the Women's Auxiliary. There also were plenty of gender-exclusive clubs for kids. The Boy Scouts and Girl Scouts. Boys Brigade and Girl Guides. Cub Scouts and Campfire Girls. And when it came to extracurricular sports, there were athletic teams for boys and cheerleading for girls. This was my world.

One day the boys in my neighborhood got together and built a tree house, and we declared it off limits to girls. We locked ourselves inside, devised passwords, and took oaths never to betray our "brothers" by divulging our secrets to females. Those were the days before political correctness took over. Men had their places and women had theirs. As I look back now, I'm struck by how counter-productive these clubs were in preparing us for life's most important club: marriage. We set ourselves apart from those of the opposite sex without realizing that we would spend the rest of our lives working to build mutually satisfying partnerships with them.

The obstacle

It doesn't matter how sexually liberated or progressive we think we are, one of the biggest obstacles men and women face—and have *always* faced—is learning to live in peace and harmony with one another. Romantic notions aside, cohabitation is challenging for both genders, which makes establishing a healthy marriage one of the most demanding and stressful adjustments in life, requiring that we rise above our natural selfishness and laziness.

The New Testament book that speaks most directly about gender issues is Paul's letter to the Ephesians; the fourth and fifth chapters in particular. Down through the centuries, this text has fueled some major battles in the war between the sexes. Irrespective of how we interpret these verses—or what we may think of Paul's take on gender roles—this passage and others like it confirm that women and men, religious or not, find it difficult to get along with each other. And marriage is the place where these difficulties are most evident. If marriage were easy, Paul would not have devoted so much ink to the subject. Thankfully, he didn't shy away from the tension and tells it like it is.

Ephesians 4:25 is a capsule of relational advice that is especially valuable in marriage: *"Therefore each of you must put off falsehood and speak truthfully to your neighbor, for we are all members of one body."* Here Paul compares Christian fellowship to membership in a club. He then takes the metaphor one step further with three little words: "of one body." Not only is the fellowship of faith a club, it is a living body, more an organism than an organization. As followers of Christ, we hold a membership in every other person who professes faith in Christ, and we are organically connected. And when two believers marry, the bond is even stronger.

Marriage and membership

Think about this. If you are a "member" of me, you might wear a T-shirt emblazoned with: "I am a member of The Richard Davis Club." And if I share your faith in Christ, I am privileged to wear a T-shirt proclaiming that I'm a member of the club bearing your name. This is part of our identity. If we love Christ, we share a new identity based on mutual love and respect, male and female alike. Because we're members of one another's club, any differences between us pale in the light of our common bond in Christ.

If this is true in Christian friendships, think of the implications for Christian marriages. When two believers stand at the altar on their wedding day, they take a public vow of membership in the "club" of their partner. But this club isn't the *institution* of marriage; it is a membership in one special *individual*. A wedding isn't an initiation into the ranks of "the married;" it is the induction into a club so exclusive that it has only two members: you and your spouse. And rather than having your partner's name stenciled on a T-shirt, this membership is recorded in a legal document, confirmed by a shared surname, displayed publicly with wedding rings, and sealed with sacred, eternal vows taken before a crowd of witnesses. This is serious stuff.

But wait a minute. There's more. Much more. In Christian marriage, the club of two members becomes a club of *three* members. It isn't just you and your spouse. As Paul says, marriage is "one body" made up of three members: you, me, and Thee. Christian marriage mirrors the Trinity, three persons in one. Two human partners and one divine: husband, wife, and Christ.

Sex...and then what?

Now, what happens when two of the members of this exclusive club don't share the same values and convictions? What will keep their club intact? There's no denying that the power of sexual attraction is strong, but can sex alone keep two people together for a lifetime? Romantic feelings come and go; they ebb and flow.

Emotions may tickle, but they're also fickle. Things can feel good one day and bad the next. Feelings are fragile and easily injured. That's why marriage can be a hotbed for hurt. And what starts hot can quickly turn cold. A marriage founded on an appetite for pleasure and nothing else is doomed to fail because lust can't produce trust.

As my wise mother used to say, "Love will get you through times without sex, but sex won't get you through times without love." If you share your body with your partner but withhold your spirit, it can't last. I've known couples that enjoy making love, but they hate making *marriage*. As their sexual pleasures start to decline—and, believe me, they always do—they find that there's little left to keep them in the marriage. Then they either search for pleasure elsewhere or slide into an attitude of resentment toward the person they are "stuck with."

Swedes and Indians

Here's something scary. Do you know there's a publication called *Divorce Magazine*?[21] I kid you not. You know your marriage is shaky when your spouse subscribes to this periodical. Not a good sign. As might be expected, among other things, *Divorce Magazine* tracks the world's divorce rates. What country do you think takes the prize for the most divorces? According to the 2002 statistics from 46 countries, it is Sweden, where 54.9% of all new marriages end in divorce. Now guess which country has the lowest divorce rate. That would be India, where only 1.1% of the couples break up. We might wonder why many more Swedes than Indians get divorced.

I have friends and church members from both Sweden and India, so I've been able to do some amateur research on my own. I am convinced that cultural values, family structure, and religious beliefs help to explain the discrepancy between Swedish and Indian divorce statistics. For example, the average Swede professes no faith in God, but the average Indian is quite religious. By all counts, Indians score much higher on marital fidelity, longevity, and

---

[21] Worldwide divorce statistics from *Divorce Magazine*:
http://www.divorcemag.com/articles/world-divorce-statistics-page-1

harmony than do Swedes. What do the Indians have that the Swedes don't? There are two obvious things:

- First, Indians have a low incidence of premarital sex compared to Swedes.
- Second, the practice of arranged marriages still exists in India today (even though it's in decline).

Our church in Zurich had several Indian couples whose marriages were arranged by their parents. For Westerners, this is unimaginable. If you tell Swedes to consider permitting their parents to pick their spouse, the response is predictable. Dismissive laughter. Ask the same of Swiss, Germans, Brits, Americans, or most other nationalities, and it's likely they will stare at you in disbelief and walk away. We in the West think of ourselves as too enlightened and liberated to entertain such archaic notions. We shop for our partners. Literally. We go shopping for them! On the internet. At bars and in singles clubs. Even at church. Then we experiment with them, trying them out by taking them for a test drive or leasing them for a few months to decide whether or not we want to make the purchase. But is our modern way necessarily better? Not if you believe the statistics.

The Book of Ephesians was written to Christians living in the Roman province of Asia Minor (Turkey today). These were people caught up in cross-cultural tensions, torn between Eastern and Western values. They had been influenced by the new, liberal philosophies of the Greeks and Romans, but their cultural roots were in the ancient traditions of the Middle East and Asia. Jesus and the early Christian evangelists were Jewish and, thus, more Eastern than Western in their views regarding marriage and family life. Because we claim to be people of the same Book, one would think we must share the same perspective on marriage as Jesus and the Jews. But do we?

Even though we in the West have inherited Greek philosophies and adopted many secular vales, our biblical roots have always been distinctively Middle Eastern. Jewish, in particular. Judaism holds marriage in the highest esteem, linking the matrimonial vows to a commitment to God. This is the sacred dimension of marriage. I am convinced that our marital problems are, at least in part, due to a breakdown in the human-divine relationship in our society. If we are no longer willing to live in loving submission to God, how likely is it that we will live in loving submission to our spouse? We shouldn't kid ourselves. Marital problems and spiritual problems are directly related. The Apostle Paul knew this two thousand years ago.

The lie about truth

Let's return to Ephesians 4:25 and use it as a template for the marriage relationship. *"Therefore each of you must put off falsehood and speak truthfully to your neighbor, for we are all members of one body."* When we enter into a close spiritual relationship with another person, we become members of something bigger than ourselves—what Scripture refers to as the "Body of Christ"—and this requires of us mutual truthfulness. If I love my wife, I am obligated to speak the truth to her with love and respect. Does this mean I should remove all filters and share with her my every thought? Should I tell her when I think she doesn't look good in a certain dress or with a new hairdo? Should I candidly tell her which other women I find attractive? Must I divulge all the things about her that turn me off? Are you kidding? If this is what God requires of husbands, He doesn't understand either women or marriage. The man who blurts out the truth even though he knows it will pierce his wife's heart isn't noble; he's stupid! He's more committed to foolishly spouting his idle thoughts than to building up his partner and loving her in Christ. There is truth, and there is loving truth. There is a difference between speaking the truth and speaking the truth in love. Every couple should know that difference.

Control vs. self-control

Several years ago, I was invited to officiate at a wedding in the Greek Islands. Before the ceremony, I pulled the bride and groom aside separately and asked them, "What is it that attracted you to the person you're about to marry?" I found it interesting that they both gave the same answer: "I was impressed by his (or her) strength and self-assurance." That prompted me to ask a second question. "What do you think will be your greatest challenge in marriage?" The bride quickly responded, "He's very stubborn, and I know that I will find that hard to live with." And the groom answered, "She's very strong-willed, and I think she's used to having her own way." Their candid answers reveal why marriage is such a challenge for all of us. Every marital problem involves a struggle for control. Marriage is the attempt to form a congenial partnership between two strong-willed individuals who each want things their own way.

While we can't know for certain if Paul the Apostle was ever married, because he was a Pharisee and marriage was a Pharisaic requirement, it is likely that at some point he had a wife. Many have speculated about this. But regardless of his domestic situation, Paul had a profound understanding of the delights and demands of marriage. His insights into the nuances of the marital union do not sound like those of a single celibate. He speaks about compassionate truthfulness and not allowing emotions to provide footholds for evil. About taming our tongues and making sure our words build up rather than put down. About speaking in a tone laced with grace. About ridding ourselves of bitterness, wrath, anger, wrangling, slander, and malice and replacing them with tenderheartedness and forgiveness. His letters are filled with wise marital counsel. Paul saw marriage as a reflection of Christ's relationship with his "bride," the Church, a relationship characterized by sacrificial love and opposed to selfish discord.

If there is a theme behind Paul's marital advice, it is that we must maintain balance and self-control at all times and never let the worst within us get the better of us. If husbands and wives did only this, divorce attorneys would soon be out of business.

The problem of having no problems

At the risk of sounding negative—which I most certainly am not when it comes to marriage—I believe there is no such thing as a problem-free marriage. Why do we think a blissful, stress-free union is even possible? Perhaps we've read too many fairy tales or romance novels. Living harmoniously with another person is a universal problem because every one of us is born self-centered. This is why I find it surprising that so many assume that inter-personal tensions are proof of a marital crisis. In fact, marital strife is normal. I believe that God invented marriage to teach us that we are not the center of the universe and to make us better people. As pastor and author Rick Warren says, "Marriage is God's way of making us holy." In most cases, we are attracted to our mate because he or she is different from us. At first, those differences are interesting and charming, but after we're married those same differences start to bother us and become points of contention. Eventually we complain to our spouse, "Why can't you do it *my* way?"

Until we realize that God has woven tension into the fabric of marriage for our own betterment, things will only get worse. Hermits and hermitesses (yes, this is a real word) may be the only ones that don't change much throughout their lives. Why is that? Because living as a recluse means not having to please anyone but yourself. If you are serious about wanting to improve as a person, here's my advice. Get married!

An Israeli friend once made this observation after visiting my country: "I think I know why you Americans have so many divorces. You haven't learned to suffer very well." How true! We'll do anything we can to avoid discomfort and suffering. But how does such avoidance make us better people? No matter how difficult it can be at times, I thank God for marriage. It provides a *purposeful suffering* that grows us up.

Let's say you have a friend who is overweight and struggling with his health. Out of concern, you urge him to consult a doctor, change his diet, and start exercising. He replies, "I've done all that, and it hasn't helped. When I adjusted my diet, I got hungry and missed my favorite foods. When I tried working out, it made me sweat and gave me sore muscles. Who needs that? There's got to be an easier way." His excuses would probably make you roll your eyes. You might tell him to 'wake up and smell the coffee' because as long as he refuses to face reality and accept that health requires hard work, his future will be grim.

It's the same with building and maintaining a healthy marriage. There are no shortcuts. Marriage requires discipline, pain, self-denial, and lots of hard work. Anyone who expects to have a good marriage without doing the hard work is living in a fantasy world.

Consider the options

Winston Churchill once said, "Democracy is the worst form of government there is...except for all the others." The same is true with many things in life. They start to look better when weighed against the alternatives. Marriage is like that. Just when you think you can't live within marriage, stop to consider the alternatives. You then may realize that it would be harder to live *without* it. Marriage is the hardest way to live...except for all the others. Don't many of the toughest things in life demand the most of us and bring out the best in us? Going through life alone may require less effort, but a lifetime partnership provides untold rewards.

For more sound marital advice, turn to 1 Peter 3:9: *"Do not repay evil with evil or insult with insult. On the contrary, repay evil with blessing, because to this you were called so that you may inherit a blessing."* Blessings don't come cheap, but when they do come, they are fantastic. Among God's most effective ways of improving us are two special relationships, one with our spouse and the other with our Creator. These are exclusive clubs with high membership dues, but what privileges and benefits they offer!

Our earthly relationship with our spouse is second in priority only to our eternal relationship with God the Father. Both are sacred and intimate unions. Ideally, marriage is the longest lasting relationship-of-choice we will experience on this side of heaven. We don't choose our parents, our siblings, or our biological children, but we do choose our mate for life. What a decision! Choose carefully and prayerfully. Then stay the course and reap the bounty.

Additional readings

The Lord God said, "It is not good for the man to be alone. I will make a helper suitable for him."

Now the Lord God had formed out of the ground all the wild animals and all the birds in the sky. He brought them to the man to see what he would name them; and whatever the man called each living creature, that was its name. So the man gave names to all the livestock, the birds in the sky and all the wild animals.

But for Adam no suitable helper was found. So the Lord God caused the man to fall into a deep sleep; and while he was sleeping, he took one of the man's ribs and then closed up the place with flesh. Then the Lord God made a woman from the rib he had taken out of the man, and he brought her to the man.

The man said, "This is now bone of my bones and flesh of my flesh; she shall be called 'woman,' for she was taken out of man." That is why a man leaves his father and mother and is united to his wife, and they become one flesh. — **Genesis 2:18-24**

I will sing of your love and justice; to you, Lord, I will sing praise.
I will be careful to lead a blameless life —
when will you come to me?
I will conduct the affairs of my house   with a blameless heart.
I will not look with approval   on anything that is vile.
I hate what faithless people do; I will have no part in it.

The perverse of heart shall be far from me; I will have nothing to do with what is evil. Whoever slanders their neighbor in secret, I will put to silence; whoever has haughty eyes and a proud heart, I will not tolerate. My eyes will be on the faithful in the land, that they may dwell with me; the one whose walk is blameless   will minister to me. No one who practices deceit   will dwell in my house; no one who speaks falsely   will stand in my presence. Every morning I will put to silence   all the wicked in the land; I will cut off every evildoer   from the city of the Lord. — **Psalm 101**

Therefore each of you must put off falsehood and speak truthfully to your neighbor, for we are all members of one body. "In your anger do not sin": Do not let the sun go down while you are still angry, and do not give the devil a foothold. Anyone who has been stealing must steal no longer, but must work, doing something useful with their own hands, that they may have something to share with those in need.

Do not let any unwholesome talk come out of your mouths, but only what is helpful for building others up according to their needs, that it may benefit those who listen. And do not grieve the Holy Spirit of God, with whom you were sealed for the day of redemption. Get rid of all bitterness, rage and anger, brawling and slander, along with every form of malice. Be kind and compassionate to one another, forgiving each other, just as in Christ God forgave you.

Follow God's example, therefore, as dearly loved children and walk in the way of love, just as Christ loved us and gave himself up for us as a fragrant offering and sacrifice to God. — **Ephesians 4:25-5:2**

Submit to one another out of reverence for Christ. Wives, submit yourselves to your own husbands as you do to the Lord. For the husband is the head of the wife as Christ is the head of the church, his body, of which he is the Savior. Now as the church submits to Christ, so also wives should submit to their husbands in everything.

Husbands, love your wives, just as Christ loved the church and gave himself up for her to make her holy, cleansing her by the washing with water through the word, and to present her to himself as a radiant church, without stain or wrinkle or any other blemish, but holy and blameless. In this same way, husbands ought to love their wives as their own bodies. He who loves his wife loves himself. After all, no one ever hated their own body, but they feed and care for their body, just as Christ does the church — for we are members of his body. "For this reason a man will leave his father and mother and be united to his wife, and the two will become one flesh." This is a profound mystery — but I am talking about Christ and the church. However, each one of you also must love his wife as he loves himself, and the wife must respect her husband. — **Ephesians 5:21-33**

Finally, all of you, be like-minded, be sympathetic, love one another, be compassionate and humble. Do not repay evil with evil or insult with insult. On the contrary, repay evil with blessing, because to this you were called so that you may inherit a blessing.

For, "Whoever would love life and see good days must keep their tongue from evil and their lips from deceitful speech. They must turn from evil and do good; they must seek peace and pursue it. For the eyes of the Lord are on the righteous and his ears are attentive to their prayer, but the face of the Lord is against those who do evil." **— 1 Peter 3:8-12**

Chapter 12
LACK OF CONFIDENCE

"I can do all this through him who gives me strength."
— **Philippians 4:13**

"One's ability to say No is closely linked to self-confidence."
— **Auliq Ice**

"Confidence is silent. Insecurities are loud." — **Source Unknown**

"No one can make you feel inferior without your consent." — **Eleanor Roosevelt**

Who is the world's most famous funambulist? Do you even know what a funambulist is? A funambulist is an aerialist, more commonly known as a tightrope walker. The most famous funambulist of all time was a Frenchman named Jean François Gravelet, whose professional moniker was "The Great Blondin." On June 30, 1859, Blondin became the first man to walk across Niagara Falls on a tightrope, and he did it in front of an audience of over 100,000 nervous spectators.

Blondin was quite a showman. Before attempting one of his many death-defying walks over the Falls, he is reputed to have inquired of the crowd, "Do you believe that I, The Great Blondin, can successfully cross high above this river on a tightrope?"

The crowd responded in unison, "We believe! We believe!"

Blondin proceeded to make his way safely to the other side. As the crowd erupted with cheers, he quickly raised his arms and silenced them. "Do you believe that I, The Great Blondin, can *again* successfully cross over the waterfalls on this tightrope—this time while pushing a wheelbarrow?"

The audience again roared with enthusiasm, "We believe! We believe! We believe!"

Blondin raised his hands to quiet them. "Then who among you is willing to sit inside this wheelbarrow and cross over with me?"

The crowd immediately fell silent. The only sound heard was the roar of the mighty Falls.

There are two morals to this story. First, it's easy to be confident when we have nothing at stake. And second, being confident in others is one thing, but entrusting our life to someone or something we can't control is a whole different matter.

Confidence and confidentiality

In the days before prosperity preachers plied their trade as motivational speakers, confidence — especially *self*-confidence — was not a common sermon topic. That may have been because the "meek and mild Lamb of God" was to be every believer's attitudinal role model, so following Jesus meant being humble. Preoccupation with self was seen as unchristian. Self-confidence, even self-consciousness, was just a step away from egotism and the dreaded sin of pride. Or so we thought. How can one be confident in Christ without becoming cocky?

Here is a paradox. Those who appear to be overflowing with confidence are often those who have little of it. Boasting is bluster that masks insecurity. As stated at the beginning of this chapter, "Confidence is silent; insecurities are loud." Ironically, a *lack* of confidence can produce a smokescreen of false arrogance and braggadocio. We are wise to remember that those who are puffed up on the outside often suffer from emptiness inside.

So what about Jesus? Was the Son of God supremely confident as he walked the earth? Or did he experience an identity crisis of his own in coming to terms with his unique calling? Within the circle of biblical scholarship is a school of thought called "process theology." Process theologians speculate that Jesus' self-awareness and sense of divine mission evolved gradually. They suggest that his confidence in God and acceptance of his sacrificial destiny wavered. Could this be true?

160

If you study the New Testament, I think you will discover that the stereotype of Jesus as an introspective, submissive mystic is inaccurate. The Jesus we encounter in the Gospel narratives is anything but timid, perplexed, or deferential. He speaks and acts like a man who is extremely self-confident. Or perhaps we should say "God-fident." I see no self-doubt in Jesus. Nor does he seem confused about his sacred mission. Even when confronted by the devil himself (in Matthew 4:1-11 and Luke 4:1-13), Jesus did not flinch or back away. Never does he give in to his critics or show concern about what others think of him. In the midst of the final week of his life, Jesus stood his ground before Caiaphas, the Sanhedrin, and Herod Antipas. As he was being interrogated by Pontius Pilate, it was Pilate who lost his nerve, not the confident Christ. The accuser was exposed by the accused.

Some say that Jesus experienced a crisis of confidence in the Garden of Gethsemane on the night of his arrest, pointing to his prayer, *"Father, if you are willing, take this cup from me."* But might this have been the normal anxiety anyone would feel in knowing that he was about to be tortured and killed? I believe it is a mistake to equate anxiety with self-doubt. Those who heard and recorded Jesus' final words — and watched him die on the cross — were profoundly moved by his unflinching confidence in God and his resolve to complete his mission.

Infectious confidence

Jesus' unwavering self-confidence in the midst of suffering and death inspired his disciples to face their own trials courageously. All but one of them fled in fear following his arrest, only to return later to rally around their resurrected master and renew their pledge of loyalty. After Christ's ascension, their confidence grew even stronger. Jesus inspired an inner courage in these men that accompanied them unto death. Peter was crucified upside down in Rome. The other apostles were executed in far off lands — all except John the Younger, who died in exile on Patmos. And many in the next wave of witnesses suffered the same fate. Stephen was stoned. The Apostle Paul, like John the Baptist, was beheaded. This sacrificial devotion has continued throughout Church history right up to today. Some who follow Christ are still suffering persecution, incarceration, and death for their faith. Is there a greater test of a person's confidence than to be willing to suffer, even die, for his or her convictions? Cowards do not martyrs make. Here is a level of confidence strong enough to overcome the deepest fears.

Hebrews 11:29-40 is one of Scripture's great confidence-builders, listing champions of the faith and the miracles God worked through them. There is Moses, who defied the world's most powerful empire to deliver his people from captivity. Joshua and Rahab, whom God used to destroy the walls of Jericho. And others, including Gideon, Barak, Samson, Jephthah, David, Samuel, and Israel's prophets. The Book of Hebrews celebrates the exploits of these giants of the faith. *"Through faith [they] conquered kingdoms, administered justice, and gained what was promised; who shut the mouths of lions, quenched the fury of the flames, and escaped the edge of the sword; whose weakness was turned to strength; and who became powerful in battle and routed foreign armies."* These feats required confidence in God *and* self-confidence, and those through whom these great deeds were accomplished had a sizable measure of both. But they were not superheroes. They had doubts and fears just as any of us would. However, they also had courage. And courage isn't the absence of fear; it is the ability to overcome fear and keep going.

The same applies to confidence. Confidence is the ability to overcome self-doubt. It is only possible to overcome a lack of self-confidence by moving beyond doubt and placing confidence in the Almighty. How is this done? By shifting our focus away from self and trusting in the supernatural power that God makes available to us.

A few verses later in Hebrews 11, the author makes a curious statement: *"Women received back their dead, raised to life again."* What does this mean? It confirms that Jesus' resurrection was not the only resurrection in Jerusalem on that first Easter weekend. According to Matthew, at the moment Christ died, *"...tombs broke open. The bodies of many holy people who had died were raised to life. They came out of the tombs after Jesus' resurrection and went into the holy city and appeared to many people."* (Matthew 27:52-

53) One has to wonder why such a startling fact is often omitted when the Easter story is told today. Knowing that many dead bodies rose to life along with Christ should boost our confidence that death is no barrier to God's will being fulfilled.

The resurrection record

There are even more physical resurrections recorded in the Bible. The prophet Elijah brings a widow's dead son back to life in 1 Kings 17:17-24. Elisha does the same for the deceased child of a Shunamite woman (2 Kings 4:8-37). Jesus restores life to the expired son of the widow of Nain (Luke 7:11-17) and repeats the miracle for Jairus' daughter (Mark 5:22-43). A short while later, Jesus performs the same miracle for his old friend Lazarus (John 11:1-46). Paul raises Eutychus from the dead in Acts 20:7-12. As one commentator wrote, "Jerusalem is the city with the highest resurrection rate in the world." No other religion or religious figure can match Christianity's resurrection record. Our God is the undisputed king of the comeback, and each comeback builds the confidence of those who believe.

Jesus did more confidence building during the hours preceding his arrest. He said this to those he would soon leave behind, *"Believe me when I say that I am in the Father and the Father is in me; or at least believe on the evidence of the works themselves. Very truly I tell you, whoever believes in me will do the works I have been doing, and they will do even greater things than these, because I am going to the Father. And I will do whatever you ask in my name, so that the Father may be glorified in the Son. You may ask me for anything in my name, and I will do it."* (John 14:11-14) This was not a mere platitude meant to bolster morale. Here was a man facing imminent torture and execution exhibiting absolute confidence in His destiny. He looked beyond the horror that awaited him and assured his friends that the best was yet to come. His pain and suffering would end once God's power was manifested and the Comforter (Holy Spirit) was revealed. This wasn't optimism; it was Jesus' complete confidence in God's ultimate triumph over nature itself.

If you have heard the Easter story so many times that it no longer moves you and has become like a fairy tale, a holiday legend or spiritual metaphor, chances are you will soon lose confidence in God. And after that, eventually in yourself. Easter is the greatest confidence builder ever. It is the antidote for misplaced expectations and broken dreams, the cure for discouragement and false confidence. Easter is our assurance that our Creator is in control.

Confidence in the midst of crisis

Perhaps another resurrection story will help. A couple years ago, a member of our church named Beth experienced a woman's worst nightmare. She and her husband Tom were expecting their first child. When the contractions came, they rushed to the hospital and were soon the proud parents of a bouncing baby boy. Friends and family gathered to celebrate. But then something went terribly wrong. Beth started to feel faint. The doctors found that she was suffering from sepsis, a potentially life-threatening infection. Things quickly went from bad to worse. They put Beth into an induced coma and prepped her for immediate surgery. When they opened her abdomen, they found that she was riddled with infection. First, her kidneys shut down. Then her liver. Next her lungs filled with fluid, and there was bleeding in her brain. Her heart rate spiked into the danger zone. Beth was in a death spiral.

I was summoned to the hospital. As soon as I arrived, I gathered her family into a circle to begin a vigil of prayer. Hour after hour we waited and prayed, prayed and waited. I made some calls to set in motion our church prayer chain. Having experienced many medical crises, I knew Beth's situation was dire. The doctors' voices and nurses' eyes were filled with doom and gloom. They knew this young mother had little chance of survival. Her problems were too severe, her decline too rapid. They tried everything, but Beth remained comatose, her vital signs flickering.

Then I did something I rarely do. I invited the medical team to step into the waiting room and join our circle of prayer. They did so without hesitation. We all grabbed hands and continued to pray. Everyone in that tight, little circle feared the worst, imagining a newborn baby being raised by a broken-hearted widower. I hate to admit it, but as we prayed for a miracle, I began to prepare mentally for Beth's funeral. I never stopped praying for healing, but I lost confidence that such a miracle was possible. Beth was so far gone that not even God could bring her back. Or so I thought.

Thankfully, there were others in our prayer circle that day whose faith was greater than mine, especially among Beth's family members. Her mother, father, husband, sister, and in-laws were all there, and they remained confident that she would survive. Not merely survive but return to full health. They prayed as if they fully expected her to resume a normal life with no after-effects, no brain damage or loss of function. As I look back now, that experience confirmed how being surrounded by confident people during a crisis can bolster our own confidence and deepen our faith. Such confidence is infectious, and confidence in Christ is a game-changer, defying all odds.

Oh, me of little faith! No sooner had we said our "amens" then the machines and monitors surrounding Beth started to flash and beep. She was still comatose, but suddenly her readings were improving. Even the doctors were baffled. Their mood shifted from cautious pessimism to guarded optimism, which is no small thing. Physicians rarely make predictions in order to avoid giving false hope, or for fear of later being accused of wrongdoing. (By the way, we clergy often exercise similar restraint.) The only ones not surprised by the sudden turn of events were Beth's family. Each new development brought smiles and nods of the head. It was as if they had expected this all along. Here were ordinary people caught up in an extraordinary trauma and yet maintaining complete confidence in God's ability to heal their loved one.

In the days that followed, the faith of Beth's friends and relatives was rewarded. She rapidly returned to full strength, so rapidly that her doctors were amazed. Her surgeon openly admitted that he had never seen a patient come so close to death and bounce back. Medical professionals rarely use words like "miracle," but that's how Beth's caregivers described her comeback. Several days later, I was visiting Beth in the hospital when two doctors stopped by to discuss her case and give their prognosis. They freely admitted having been deeply impressed by the family's faith. Beth's inexplicable recovery had expanded their confidence in God. They had witnessed invisible forces taking over where their expertise stopped, and it made an impact.

This episode taught me a lesson: Never let a lack of confidence define the possibilities. This is especially true with transcendent possibilities. As Jesus said, *"What is impossible with man is possible with God."* (Luke 18:27) Just because we are shaky and full of doubt doesn't mean everyone is. When we are nervous or skeptical, we should seek out people with unshakable convictions, for they live in a realm where odds and statistics are meaningless. Faith and confidence are not bound by such limitations.

Several weeks later, I asked Beth to share her story with our congregation during worship. It was Easter Sunday, the perfect occasion to hear from someone who had experienced her own resurrection. Beth's eloquent message gave us all a great boost of confidence and made us wonder what God might do for any of us when help is needed. Experiencing a miracle isn't essential for belief, but it sure helps to build confidence in our own faith.

The journey of spiritual descent

Miracle stories alone are not enough to convince hardcore doubters that God intervenes in our lives. They dismiss such things as coincidental or random and stubbornly refuse to believe. And there are others who say, "Okay, God may do special things for certain people, but I'm not one of them. Nothing miraculous ever happens in my life." Even regular churchgoers can be dubious and lose their confidence in supernatural intervention. It's often when trouble hits that spiritual vulnerability is exposed.

When problems arise that can't be solved by our natural resources, we find ourselves standing on wobbly legs at the edge of a slippery slope. The first thing we feel is loss of control, which is delusional because we never have as much control as we think we do. But this feeling of helplessness causes an erosion of confidence that can result in panic and despair.

Here's how the slide down the slippery slope happens. As we start to sense our own resources are inadequate to sustain or save us, we become anxious. We don't know where to turn. Our composure goes into free fall. We lose confidence in self. Then we become skeptical, and our skepticism hardens into cynicism. Once cynicism sets in, the next downward step is agnosticism. And, after that, atheism. Finally, we descend into nihilism[22] and fatalism, where meaning evaporates, hope is lost, and despair reigns. This downward spiritual spiral happens surprisingly quickly, and it begins with the loss of confidence. Depicted as a descending stairway, it looks like this:

The failure of reason and loss of control...

> **leads to loss of confidence...**

> **leads to skepticism...**

> **leads to cynicism...**

> **leads to agnosticism...**

> **leads to atheism...**

> **leads to nihilism...**

> **leads to fatalism...**

> **leads to despair.**

Each change in attitude drags us deeper down into a place where faith is shrouded in darkness. We lose our sense of God's presence and see no evidence of God, finding it hard to believe that He ever cared. God is not here. He is not there. It feels like He's no longer *anywhere*.

---

[22] Nihilism is the view (or belief) that traditional values and morals are unfounded and subjective and existence is senseless and meaningless.

Losing our religion

As we find that everything we have relied on previously no longer helps us to cope or manage our lives, we become disillusioned and disheartened. The rock group R.E.M. pondered this spiritual dilemma in their 1991 chart-topping lament titled *Losing My Religion*. The lyrics describe a loss of confidence that is both internal and *eternal*. This could be the theme song for all those who have taken the dark, dangerous plunge into despair.

Here in the Western World, and perhaps elsewhere, we are told that people are losing their religion in unprecedented numbers. Before reaching any conclusions, let's recognize the distinction between religion and faith. They are not the same. Religion is comprised of human-created systems that try to organize and control those who look to God for meaning in their lives. Faith, on the other hand, is the hope and love found in the hearts of those who have an ongoing relationship with God and have entrusted their lives to Him. Religion is external and institutional. Faith is internal and relational. In light of this, losing one's religion may not be such a bad thing. In fact, it may actually be a good thing if it clears the way for intimacy with the Almighty. It is the loss of *faith* that is far more serious because it brings with it a loss of confidence in God, which, in turn, accelerates the loss of self-confidence. It is a double-edged sword that's lethal to the soul.

If you no longer sense God's presence in your life, it's time to take inventory. Is it that you are disillusioned with *religion*? Or is it something more? Losing the desire to go to church, or join a Christian community, may or may not be a sign that you are losing your faith. That's for you to answer. But if you do not sense God's presence in your life, it may be that a loss of confidence has thrown your spirit out of whack. God is no longer on your radar screen because your radar is broken.

Loss of expectations and loss of confidence

I have found that when I no longer expect God to reveal Himself, He seems to disappear. Strange how that happens. I stop hearing His voice. I find other explanations for what's happening around me. I develop a bad attitude, feel sorry for myself, and become impatient and short-tempered. These are signs that there is an ever-widening gap between God and myself. When I lose my confidence, I also lose my interest in community, and that leads to isolation. Fortunately, I have learned to see this coming and can nip it in the bud. But I must remain vigilant.

As I consider the state of affairs in our world, I wonder if our loss of confidence in God — and in authority in general — has left our society in disarray. This includes the public's loss of confidence in the Church. Even those of us who profess faith may be giving lip service to religion but failing to live as if faith matters. It's all part of the same package. If we refuse to submit to God's authority, in whom or what do we place our confidence?

The author Marianne Williamson gives an eloquent definition of confidence:

> *"You are a child of God. Your playing small does not serve the world. There is nothing enlightened about shrinking so that people won't feel insecure around you. You were born to make manifest the glory of God that is within us. It's not just in some of us; it's in all of us. And when we let our own light shine, we unconsciously give other people permission to do the same. As we are liberated from our own fear, our presence automatically liberates others."* [23]

Ms. Williams makes the point that by devaluing ourselves (or our God), we reduce the space for others around us to grow, and we stifle their aspirations and enthusiasm. But if we remain confident and secure, those folks may catch some confidence and security for themselves.

---

[23] Marianne Williamson, *A Return To Love: Reflections on the Principles of a Course in Miracles*, Harper Collins, 1992, Chapter 7, Section 3 (pp. 190-191).

Our society gives mixed messages about confidence. Self-appointed gurus work to inflate our egos, while advertisers strive to fuel our insecurities for their own profit. As has been said, "If you put a small value upon yourself, rest assured that the world will not raise your price." We should not allow others to define our value. Not our family. Not our peers. Not our teachers or coaches. Not our friends. And certainly not strangers. Regardless of what the self-help books tell us, no person is qualified to place a value on us. Nor can we do it ourselves. Our Maker is the only one qualified to decide what we are worth.

Pathological confidence vs. Christ-centered confidence

Philippians 4:13 may be the Bible's definitive word on confidence. It is Paul's great boast in Christ. *"I can do all this through him who gives me strength."* Paul, the reformed cynic and persecutor of the faith—who was once pathologically self-confident himself—was knocked off his high horse when Jesus appeared to him in a vision. The encounter shattered his self-assurance and brought him to his knees, humbling him and drawing him into a relationship with Christ. In the days that followed, his hubris evaporated and was replaced with a newfound confidence and spiritual balance. Isn't this what every prideful and rigid spirit needs? A breakdown followed by a remake.

We are surrounded by hucksters who prey upon our insecurities to sell us their wares. "Pay our modest fee," they tell us, "and we'll give you self-assurance, self-actualization, and boundless success!" But they are peddling cockiness, not confidence. Compared to a genuine relationship with God, their promises are vain and empty. Their road to self-reliance is a dead end. On our own we can do nothing. Nothing! But *"in Christ"* we can do anything. Anything! As we place our confidence in God, our insecurities evaporate, and His infinite strength fills us. This is the same strength that moved the heaviest stone in the universe on that Easter morning 2,000 years ago, and it can remove our heaviest burdens just as easily.

In the same way that the Great Blondin invited a volunteer to climb into his wheelbarrow and ride across the raging river, Christ invites us to place our confidence in him and allow him to carry us the *full distance*, from this side of life to the other. Any takers?

Additional readings

For by the grace given me I say to every one of you: Do not think of yourself more highly than you ought, but rather think of yourself with sober judgment, in accordance with the faith God has distributed to each of you. — **Romans 12:3**

In all my prayers for all of you, I always pray with joy because of your partnership in the gospel from the first day until now, being confident of this, that he who began a good work in you will carry it on to completion until the day of Christ Jesus. — **Philippians 1:4-6**

I know what it is to be in need, and I know what it is to have plenty. I have learned the secret of being content in any and every situation, whether well fed or hungry, whether living in plenty or in want. I can do all this through him who gives me strength.
— **Philippians 4:12-13**

By faith the people passed through the Red Sea as on dry land; but when the Egyptians tried to do so, they were drowned. By faith the walls of Jericho fell, after the army had marched around them for seven days. By faith the prostitute Rahab, because she welcomed the spies, was not killed with those who were disobedient.
And what more shall I say? I do not have time to tell about Gideon, Barak, Samson and Jephthah, about David and Samuel and the prophets, who through faith conquered kingdoms, administered justice, and gained what was promised; who shut the mouths of lions, quenched the fury of the flames and escaped the edge of the sword;
whose weakness was turned to strength; and who became powerful in battle and routed foreign armies. Women received back their dead, raised to life again.

There were others who were tortured, refusing to be released so that they might gain an even better resurrection. Some faced jeers and flogging, and even chains and imprisonment. They were put to death by stoning; they were sawed in two; they were killed by the sword. They went about in sheepskins and goatskins, destitute, persecuted and mistreated — the world was not worthy of them. They wandered in deserts and mountains, living in caves and in holes in the ground.
These were all commended for their faith, yet none of them received what had been promised, since God had planned something better for us so that only together with us would they be made perfect.

— Hebrews 11:29-40

Chapter 13
FINANCIAL ANXIETY

"No one can serve two masters. Either you will hate the one and love the other, or you will be devoted to the one and despise the other. You cannot serve both God and money." — **Matthew 6:24**

"As much money and life as you could want! The two things most human beings would choose above all. The trouble is, humans do have a knack of choosing precisely those things that are worst for them."
— **J. K. Rowling**

"Too many people spend money they haven't earned, to buy things they don't want, to impress people that they don't like." — **Will Rogers**

Before our children were born, Susan and I made the commitment to train them in the habit of giving. Our plan was to teach them to tithe (give 10% of their income to support God's work) and provide for them opportunities to share with others a portion of their own money. Every Sunday during our years in Belfast, we gave the kids a 10 pence (10p) coin to drop in the offering plate at church. It was a weekly practice we hoped would instill in them the discipline of stewardship.

One Sunday I found that I had no 10p coins, so I gave Ben and Sarah a 20 pence (20p) coin each for their Sunday school offering. On our way home after church, we stopped at a store to pick up some items for lunch. Ben came in the shop with me, and as I was paying the cashier, he ran up and dropped a couple pieces of candy on the counter.

"No candy today, Ben," I told him, "not before lunch."

"It's OK, Dad," he said, "I'll pay for it myself." He then handed a 10p coin to the checkout lady.

This caught me by surprise, so I asked Ben, age eight, where he had gotten the money.

He smiled and answered proudly, "I got it from the offering at church. I put in 20p and took back my 10p in change."

Rather than being impressed by my son's math ability, I was troubled that my lessons in charity had been ineffective. And then an even more frightening thought occurred to me. What did Ben's Sunday school teacher think of the pastor's son being a moneychanger in the house of God? Fuel for the fires of church gossip.

As Ben saw it, he had met his weekly 10p obligation to God, so the rest was all his. Pennies from heaven. When it comes to making a buck, Ben isn't the only one who is an opportunist. Most of us know generosity is a virtue, but when temptations arise our conscience is compromised. We instinctively find ways to invest the least to acquire the most and give small portions to others while keeping more for ourselves.

God's hand in our pockets

Throughout my years in the pulpit, I have rarely preached about money because I know that my profession is frequently criticized for solicitous sermonizing. Among those who rarely go to church, this is the excuse-of-choice. But this criticism reveals more about the critic than the preacher. Money has a way of exposing the contents of the heart. It's easy to appear generous without ever giving God access to our assets. We diligently protect our own pockets, and in a world ruled by mammon, those who preach generosity are seen as meddlers.

Like it or not, the Bible contains more references to money (gold, silver, mammon, materialism, wealth, etc.) than any other subject, including faith, hope, and love. Given that, instead of being proud of how rarely I speak on the subject, perhaps I should blush. Shame on me for avoiding one of Scripture's hottest topics! Might this chapter help me atone for my sin of omission? We'll see.

Both the Old and New Testaments give specific instructions for godly money management. Since the only Bible Jesus knew was the Torah (the Christian Old Testament), the roots of his teachings are in the ancient Jewish legal codes. For example, Jesus says in Matthew 5:17, *"Do not think that I have come to abolish the Law or the Prophets; I have not come to abolish them but to fulfill them."* This is one of many passages where he adds clarity to a familiar text. Jesus interpreted the Jewish Scriptures for an audience that had been influenced by Gentile (secular) values. Building bridges of cross-cultural understanding is especially difficult when it comes to religion and fiscal matters. Some basic knowledge about Judaism is essential before applying biblical principles to our current socio-economic environment. It's complicated.

Using money and usury money

A good place to begin is Deuteronomy 23:19-20. Here, and in the verses that follow, we find a template for a just and efficient economic system. *"Do not charge a fellow Israelite interest, whether on money or food or anything else that may earn interest. You may charge a foreigner interest, but not a fellow Israelite, so that the Lord your God may bless you in everything you put your hand to in the land you are entering to possess."* Some translations replace "a fellow Israelite" with the broader term "brother," but the use of the term "foreigner" in the next verse suggests there are different rules for insiders than for outsiders. As we apply this text to our situation, let's substitute the word "insider" for "Israelite" and "outsider" for "foreigner." Now the passage can be seen as forbidding the charging of interest to those within our own community, while allowing for charging interest on loans made to strangers. Since Scripture consistently opposes fiscal abuse and injustice, it's safe to assume that overcharging of any kind is strictly forbidden. This is known as **usury**. And God forbids usury.[24] The problem is: The Bible doesn't define what is a "fair"

---

[24] http://dictionary.reference.com/browse/usury

rate of interest, which leaves plenty of room for finding loopholes. And when it comes to our own finances, aren't we all looking for loopholes?

In the U.S. and Western Europe in recent years, the average interest rate charged on credit cards and loans has vacillated between 7% and 36%.[25] Based on biblical standards, do these rates qualify as usury? I believe they do. However, if we look at countries like Brazil or Malawi—where interest rates on lending average between 20% and 50%—we find that the definition of usury can be relative.[26] Compared to the interest Americans and Europeans pay on loans, such rates are extortion. What must God think about the inner-workings of our global markets? It's hard to know. Ours is an economy where prices fluctuate according to what the markets will bear, so making judgments based on Scripture in the midst of such economic variables is a dodgy business.

Susan and I have owned homes in America and Switzerland. I remember when U.S. mortgage rates soared above 15% in the early 1980s. I also remember rates dropping below 5% only a few years later. But then we were spoiled by the Swiss banking system with its mortgage rates of less than 1%. Can you see why we wince at paying California interest rates? One person's financial parity is another's disparity. What we consider reasonable depends on what we're used to. As the saying goes, "once the dog has slept in the kitchen, he won't sleep outside again." Comfort brings with it complacency and entitlement. And what is fair in one setting is thievery in another. However, comparisons don't release us from accountability when it comes to practicing justice, charity, and mercy in all that we do. Market rates fluctuate, but divine standards do not.

Nowhere in Scripture is charging interest forbidden. Nor is it strongly endorsed. But taking advantage of others to gain more

---

[25] http://en.wikipedia.org/wiki/Credit_card_interest

[26] http://data.worldbank.org/indicator/FR.INR.LEND/countries

for self is clearly a violation of God's will. Self-serving financial schemes that cause others to suffer are immoral. And it's even worse when those taken advantage of are left to teeter on the edge of poverty. A biblical approach to money management may be of little interest to the public in general, but there are principles that every person of faith should practice habitually. For example, the Book of Proverbs gives basic advice for the handling of money, showing there are right and wrong ways of doing business and condemning unrestrained greed. The consequences are disastrous both to individuals and to society.

We don't have to look far to see the damage done by rampant usury. We have recently witnessed the fallout within our own economy. The credit crisis of 2008 exposed how the greedy feed on the needy. The so-called masters of the marketplace became intoxicated on their lust for riches. They fabricated debt packages and manipulated interest rates to lure the masses into economic traps. Imagine how things would have played out differently if the financial establishment had stuck to biblical principles. Had wiser heads and more ethical hearts ruled, it's likely the disaster would have been averted.

Financial finger-pointing

While it's easy to point fingers at those who rule the financial roost, we should acknowledge our own part in these things. In Deuteronomy 23:21-23, we read, *"If you make a vow to the Lord your God, do not be slow to pay it, for the Lord your God will certainly demand it of you and you will be guilty of sin. But if you refrain from making a vow, you will not be guilty. Whatever your lips utter you must be sure to do, because you made your vow freely to the Lord your God with your own mouth."* What does it mean to make a vow? And what does this have to do with charging interest? More than we may think. When we sign a contract, take out a loan, or use a credit card, we make a pledge of honor to pay back the amount borrowed. While it's easy to accuse the rich of taking advantage of the poor, there is no excuse for knowingly allowing others to take advantage of *us*. We shouldn't blame others for *our* bad decisions. Engaging in abusive usury is wrong for creditors and debtors alike. Every transaction requires at least two parties. I learned long ago that the wealthy do not have a monopoly on greed. Anyone is susceptible to avarice. Greed is not determined by how much we possess but by what possesses us.

As we consider the Bible's teachings, we encounter this inescapable reality: It is impossible to over-estimate the power money can have on the human heart. Jesus spoke of this often and warned that it is wrong to draw spiritual conclusions based on an individual's financial status.

Rich materially = poor spiritually?

In some religious circles, the rich are thought to be spiritually impoverished, as if there is an inverse correlation between personal wealth and spiritual health. Whether we admit it or not, many of us assume that worldly affluence is incompatible with godly influence. And this feeds the belief that we must adopt a lifestyle of austerity — even poverty — in order to be rich in spirit. This is known as *asceticism*, a philosophy that has influenced Judaism, Christianity, and most other religions. The fact is, religious asceticism brings with it controversy and conflict. It is easy to construct what seems to be a sound argument against accumulating wealth if we take certain Bible verses out of context. It's unfair to use carefully selected texts to support the assumption that someone's outer condition reveals his or her inner condition. Jesus and the prophets warned that this practice feeds self-righteousness.

There is an even more dangerous assumption that comes with equating the external with the internal. Namely, that material blessings are proof of divine blessing. This false correlation has birthed many heresies known by many names: the prosperity gospel, the health and wealth gospel, the name-it-and-claim-it gospel, the blessing of the blessed…to name just a few. Prosperity preachers oppose the practice of shedding worldly trappings to prove devotion to God. They preach a message of anti-asceticism. Ironically, both asceticism and prosperity theology are based on the same assumption: that worldliness and godliness are intrinsically linked. Both doctrines are equally false.

Where does this leave us? If spiritual health and worldly wealth are not intertwined, where do we find balance? And if godly living doesn't guarantee material blessings, what are the results of *ungodly* living? One tenable answer is found in Matthew 5:45, where Jesus says that our heavenly Father *"causes His sun to rise on the evil and the good, and sends rain on the righteous and the unrighteous."* While this may not reduce the tension in trying to maintain spiritual health in a material world, it certainly discourages us from reducing life's complexities to a set of simplistic assumptions.

I know many wealthy people who consistently share their abundance with those who have less. And most of them give quietly because they are spiritually mature. They know that the highest form of giving is done in private, even anonymously. While we are right in commending those of modest means who share the little they have, in reality, no charitable organization can survive without the generosity of at least a few large donors. The generosity of the rich few helps to keep the struggling many afloat. If we resent the wealthy simply because they possess wealth, we commit the sin of judging others without seeing the bigger picture.

The larger the target, the more tempting it is to take potshots. This is especially true when it comes to those who sit at the pinnacle of wealth and power. In Luke 12:48, Jesus says, *"From everyone who has been given much, much will be demanded; and from the one who has been entrusted with much, much more will be asked."* Do we think Jesus was referring to the rich and powerful here and not to ordinary folks like us? These words were directed at **ALL** of us, regardless of the size of our bank accounts. Each of us should consider what God has entrusted to us—in whatever measure—and then decide how best to share a portion of those blessings with others. While it's true that "fat cats" are big targets, do we think those of us with fewer assets are less visible to God? And are we less accountable? Remember that not all gifts are material in nature. Consider the other blessings: talent, free time, intelligence, compassion, speaking or teaching skills, organizational and administrative capabilities, and countless other assets and resources. God bestows a wide variety of blessings upon His children; so why get hung up on the more obvious ones? Even a one-trick pony is expected to exercise his single trick to the fullest…and for the benefit and betterment of others.

Faith, farming, and finances

I'd like us to return to Deuteronomy 23 before I wrap up this chapter. Verses 24-25: *"If you enter your neighbor's vineyard, you may eat all the grapes you want, but do not put any in your basket. If you enter your neighbor's grain field, you may pick kernels with your hands, but you must not put a sickle to their standing grain."* What are we to make of this? Is it merely folksy advice given to our agrarian ancestors, or does it have something to do with our own financial context? I believe there is a universal principle here.

As God's people, we are to have a "what's-mine-is-yours" attitude instead of a preoccupation with acquiring more and protecting what we have. As we go about our daily business and tend to our own "harvest," we're told to be constantly ready to come to the aid of those whose crops have failed. Caring for others means *sharing* with others, whether it's grapes, grain, groceries, gifts, or anything else. If we keep our storehouse loaded and locked tight, we run the risk of being imprisoned by our wealth.

There is another aspect of this scenario. If our storehouse is empty, we should be willing to graciously accept the help of those who have more without ever taking advantage of them. Poverty is often accompanied by self-pity and the expectation that those with more should ante up for those with less. Just as the rich sometimes take advantage of the poor, the poor sometimes take advantage of the rich by claiming they are entitled to charity. After all, isn't it a given that those with much should provide for those with less? Not so fast! This may be true in a perfect world, but not in an imperfect world, where doling out charity tends to stifle motivation and breed dependency. Unfortunately, the best intentions can produce the worst results. Charity distributed unwisely undermines the self-respect of the one receiving the help and can result in an attitude of resignation causing laziness. According to Deuteronomy 23, we may gratefully accept a few morsels, but we shouldn't strip our neighbors' vines of all the fruit and pile it in our own storehouse. Take a drink, yes, but don't drain the whole barrel. Too much of a good thing can be bad, both in giving and receiving. With maturity comes moderation.

We live in a society drunk on mammon. We indulge in vice while ignoring God's *advice*. We are spoiled. One generation's luxury is the next generation's necessity. Having grown up at a time of unprecedented abundance and opportunity, we 21st centurions have been conditioned to think we deserve certain things. This is simply wrong. We have not been given a certificate of entitlement, so why do we act like we have? In truth, we deserve nothing! *Everything* we have is a gift from the Creator, and once we accept this, our attitude toward money and possessions is radically transformed. Suddenly giving becomes far more exciting than receiving, and we lose the urge to take away from others. Contentment with what we have (or *don't* have) causes us to see beyond the ephemeral and invest in the eternal. As the things of this world become less important to us, our appetites and aspirations change, and we begin to see that life is relational rather than transactional.

When it comes down to it, there are two surefire ways to measure people's priorities. Look at their schedule and their bank statements. But before examining others, first examine yourself. Look at your own calendar and financial ledgers. How are *you* spending your time and money? If you answer that question honestly, you will discover who owns your mind, heart, and soul.

One final word on this subject...

As I was discussing this chapter with trusted friends, several suggested I say more about tithing and offer advice for personal budgeting, asset management, and financial accountability. Some even thought I should explain various economic theories and models. I considered this advice but decided not to stray beyond my field of interest and expertise.

I am anything but a financial guru, so I think it wise to leave financial advising to the experts. My purpose is not to offer guidelines for managing money. First, I don't believe there is one right way to do this. Every situation is unique. Second, others have written well — and abundantly — on these topics. If you wish to go further, I suggest doing some research on your own. There are literally thousands of resources out there. If you're looking for a good introductory book on godly money management, check out these authors: Larry Burkett, Austin Pryor, Dave Ramsey, Mary Hunt, Ron Blue, and Howard Dayton.

My best advice for managing money is something I learned from working my first paper route as a kid: "If you can't afford it, don't buy it!" Isn't it amazing how this simple nugget of wisdom has passed the test of time? It is a truism that cures many ills and rights many wrongs. I practice it still.

Additional readings

All these blessings will come on you and accompany you if you obey the Lord your God: You will be blessed in the city and blessed in the country. The fruit of your womb will be blessed, and the crops of your land and the young of your livestock — the calves of your herds and the lambs of your flocks. Your basket and your kneading trough will be blessed. You will be blessed when you come in and blessed when you go out.

The Lord will grant that the enemies who rise up against you will be defeated before you. They will come at you from one direction but flee from you in seven. The Lord will send a blessing on your barns and on everything you put your hand to. The Lord your God will bless you in the land he is giving you. The Lord will establish you as his holy people, as he promised you on oath, if you keep the commands of the Lord your God and walk in obedience to him. Then all the peoples on earth will see that you are called by the name of the Lord, and they will fear you.

The Lord will grant you abundant prosperity — in the fruit of your womb, the young of your livestock and the crops of your ground — in the land he swore to your ancestors to give you. The Lord will open the heavens, the storehouse of his bounty, to send rain on your land in season and to bless all the work of your hands. You will lend to many nations but will borrow from none.

The Lord will make you the head, not the tail. If you pay attention to the commands of the Lord your God that I give you this day and carefully follow them, you will always be at the top, never at the bottom.
— **Deuteronomy 28:2-13**

Honor the Lord with your wealth, with the firstfruits of all your crops; then your barns will be filled to overflowing, and your vats will brim over with new wine. — **Proverbs 3:9-10**

To the person who pleases him, God gives wisdom, knowledge and happiness, but to the sinner he gives the task of gathering and storing up wealth to hand it over to the one who pleases God. This too is meaningless, a chasing after the wind. — **Ecclesiastes 2:26**

Bring the whole tithe into the storehouse, that there may be food in my house. Test me in this," says the Lord Almighty, "and see if I will not throw open the floodgates of heaven and pour out so much blessing that there will not be room enough to store it. I will prevent pests from devouring your crops, and the vines in your fields will not drop their fruit before it is ripe," says the Lord Almighty. "Then all the nations will call you blessed, for yours will be a delightful land," says the Lord Almighty. — **Malachi 3:10-12**

"Do not judge, and you will not be judged. Do not condemn, and you will not be condemned. Forgive, and you will be forgiven. Give, and it will be given to you. A good measure, pressed down, shaken together and running over, will be poured into your lap. For with the measure you use, it will be measured to you." — **Luke 6:37-38**

Remember this: Whoever sows sparingly will also reap sparingly, and whoever sows generously will also reap generously. Each of you should give what you have decided in your heart to give, not reluctantly or under compulsion, for God loves a cheerful giver. And God is able to bless you abundantly, so that in all things at all times, having all that you need, you will abound in every good work. — **2 Corinthians 9:6-8**

Chapter 14
SPIRITUAL MEDIOCRITY

"But why diminish your soul being run-of-the-mill at something? Mediocrity: now there is ugliness for you. Mediocrity's a hairball coughed up on the Persian carpet of Creation."
— **Tom Robbins**, *Half Asleep in Frog Pajamas*

"We don't want to think about our weaknesses. We don't want to talk about them, and we certainly don't want anyone else to point them out. This is a classic sign of mediocrity, and this mediocrity has a firm grip on the Church and humanity at this moment in history."
— **Matthew Kelly**, *Rediscover Catholicism*

"Nothing is good but mediocrity. The majority has settled that, and finds fault with him who escapes it at whichever end."
— **Blaise Pascal**, *Pensées*

"I know your deeds, that you are neither cold nor hot. I wish you were either one or the other! So, because you are lukewarm — neither hot nor cold — I am about to spit you out of my mouth." — **Revelation 3:15-16**

Before tackling this topic, I should explain what I mean by "spiritual mediocrity" and why I think it is an issue for people today. As a framework for our discussion, I offer the following points:

- It is generally accepted that there are three basic dimensions (aspects or spheres) to our humanity: the physical, the mental/emotional, and the spiritual. Because the spiritual self transcends physicality and consciousness, it is the most difficult to comprehend or prove. However, every aspect of our personhood was designed by the Creator to be both distinctive and inter-related. If we want to be whole and healthy, we need to give at least as much attention to our spirit as we do to our body and mind.

- As with any slow-developing physical or mental illness, we can also slip into spiritual illness without knowing it. I liken it to being jaded. We become numb to the spiritual messages deep within us to the point that we are desensitized and fall into a permanent state of apathy. This happens with many things in life: food, drink, sex, drugs, emotional highs, relationships, even fun and recreation. My late grandmother's advice for me before our first move to Europe was, "Take lots of pictures during your first few weeks there because what at first seems exotic soon becomes commonplace." Well put, Gram. In a similar way, once we lose our delight in the small wonders around and within us, our spirit starts to wither, leaving us feeling disillusioned and empty.

- When it comes to sensory stimulation, never have so many been exposed to so much for so long as we are today. Ours is a generation addicted to amusement and sensation. The same is true of our spiritual appetite, which may explain why so many religious organizations feel the need to keep upping the emotional ante to hold people's attention and engender their devotion. We see this in many mega-churches with their penchant for trendiness and bedazzlement. Their worship productions bombard the congregation with sights and sounds, entertaining messages, and formulas for finding happiness. Compare this methodology to Judaism's age-old disciplines. Jewish rituals have always been practiced primarily within the home, with big religious events happening only a few times each year. Many Christian churches now feel the need to provide scintillating worship weekly—if not even more often—in hopes of attracting new members while also holding the attention of their older members.

- At the other end of the spectrum is institutional religion, which can be so mired in ritualism that there is no room for anything new or fresh. When a church falls into stale and stagnant institutionalism, vitality is squelched and opportunities are lost. To anyone who cares about internal — and *eternal* — health, lifeless religiosity should be a grave concern.

Metaphysical mediocrity?

The deeper we delve into the mysteries of creation, the more we see that nothing in the cosmos is wasted. Not in the microcosm nor in the macrocosm. Regardless of how much we do or don't understand of nature's mysteries, how can we not be awed by what we see around us every day? How privileged we are to be a part of such a complex, boundless universe! And if this is true in the natural realm, it's even truer in the *super*natural realm. The more we see of the intricacy and efficiency of the universe, the more we suspect there must be a Mastermind behind this cosmic masterpiece.

Scientific evidence suggests that the small reflects the large in the natural realm. Might this also be true in the supernatural realm? If the Bible's claim of supernatural inspiration is true, even the linguistic details in the text may provide insights into its Author. This is the premise behind the hermeneutical school of textual criticism, where every jot and tittle of Scripture is worth analyzing because it may reveal something bigger. This is why we should pay special attention to the frequency particular words are used within the text. Why are some words used only once and others are used repeatedly? This is an important question if smaller things reveal bigger things.

For example, the word "lukewarm" appears only once in the Bible. Revelation 3:15-16 says, *"I know your deeds, that you are neither cold nor hot. I wish you were either one or the other! So, because you are **lukewarm** – neither hot nor cold – I am about to spit you out of my mouth."* The Greek word that the author John uses here is *chliaros*, which refers to a temperature somewhere between hot and cold. Why did John choose this specific word to describe spiritual mediocrity? Given that this is the only time the word is used in all of Scripture, it begs investigation.

Tepid troubles

John's vision was originally recorded and sent to seven first-century congregations in ancient Asia Minor, what is now western

Turkey. This is an area abundant in one resource more valuable than oil. Water! The general public is unaware that water is a primary reason why Turkey will continue to occupy a pivotal position for the European Union and Middle East in the foreseeable future. The Turks control 90% of the fresh water in that part of the world. Oil is money, but water is *life*. Without oil, engines stop running. Without water, we all stop running! All the more reason to keep our eyes on Turkey in the coming days.

John had water in mind as he wrote about the congregation in the ancient city of Laodicea in his apocalyptic vision in the Book of Revelation. He compared the quality of the local church to the quality of the local water. The New International Version gives a translation of Revelation 3:16 that is especially vivid: *"So, because you are lukewarm — neither cold nor hot — I am about to spit you out of my mouth."* John was troubled by the spiritual illness he had witnessed in the church. And since sick people are prone to vomiting, this is the verb John uses to describe their illness. However, it was not the congregants he saw vomiting but someone else. Because John claims to speak on behalf of Jesus (see Revelation 1:9-11), this is the Lord's admission that spiritual mediocrity makes him sick to his stomach. Quite graphic, wouldn't you say?

Susan and I have visited the ancient city of Laodicea twice to tour its ruins and learn its history. Prior to those visits, I hadn't realized that ancient Laodicea had long been known as "The Lukewarm City." The old Greek name for the nearby river—which today is the Lycus River—was the River Lukos (pronounced "liukos," in Greek, Λύκος). The locals knew this was a "Lukos-warm" river because its water flowed into their city through stone pipes from the hot springs located in Pamukkale, four miles away. By the time it reached them, it was merely warm, which made it awful to drink but perfect for the city's famous spas. The water also contained so much calcium that not only did it taste bad, it clogged the plumbing system, forcing the city's engineers to place vents along the main pipeline to allow for regular maintenance.

This is a ton of background information, but it is essential for understanding John's warning to the Laodicean church. And to us! These things happen in many churches...past, present, or future. John saw the Laodicean water system as a metaphor for the Laodicean congregation. Just as the city's pipes contained lukewarm water, the church contained lukewarm spirituality. The tepid water felt good but tasted bad. Worse yet, it was damaging the infrastructure. Had the water been colder, the sludge wouldn't have accumulated so quickly. Had it been hotter, the steam would have killed the microorganisms clogging the pipes. Lukewarm water promotes the growth of substances that jeopardize human health. Were it not for the diligence of the Laodicean water department, the population would have been deathly sick. But what protection is there for lukewarm faith?

This passage is about more than the quality of the water in an obscure, ancient village. It's a warning to all who profess faith in Jesus Christ. John wanted all believers to know that something dangerous can pollute Christian fellowship, making the members vulnerable to illness. The Scottish Bible commentator William Barclay describes Laodicea as a thriving center of finance and industry, to such an extent that the city refused Roman aid. The Laodiceans preferred relying on their own resources rather than being dependent on the empire.[27] Sound familiar? Laodicea was the ancient equivalent of our own society. We too have grown prosperous on the local resources and been lulled into self-reliance. Little do we know how thin our veneer of false security really is.

Let's take the comparison one step further. We know that Laodicea was one of the leading medical centers in Asia Minor, much like the centers of the health care industry in today's world. Outsiders came from far and wide seeking healing. The significance of this wasn't lost on John. He saw in Laodicea universal warning signs. This is why his vision is relevant to

---

[27] *The Revelation of John, Volume 1* by William Barclay, The Westminster Press, 1976, p. 138.

believers two millennia later. Many are still at risk of becoming "not so hot."

Intoxicated on comfort

Why should any of this matter to us? Even though lukewarm Christianity may not concern you, please stay with me here. The very things that make a community lazy and complacent can do the same within its individual members. And this can affect the health of an entire society. John's condemnation of the Laodiceans was less about their lack of emotional fervor and more about their ineffectiveness at bringing God's kingdom into this world. It wasn't that their worship was lukewarm—even though that may have been true—it was that they had become lukewarm in attitude. John says nothing about their worship services but instead addresses their failure to live out their faith. Their worship may have, in fact, been vibrant, but they were ineffective in ministering to those around them for Christ's sake.

Spiritual spas

When Susan and I lived in Zurich, we would occasionally drive to a nearby spa called Bad Ragaz for a day of indulging in the natural hot springs. ("Bad" is pronounced "Baud" in German, meaning "bath.") It was fantastic. We lounged in the pools, being massaged by water jets and basking in the warm humidity. It was the ultimate stress relief. After a few hours of this, we became wrinkly and pinkly prunes. Happy prunes. As we stepped out of the water, the staff would wrap us in toasty towels and escort us to a warm, quiet room for a nap. For us, it wasn't Bad Ragaz; it was *Good* Ragaz. *Very Good* Ragaz!

Guess what we loved most about our time at the spa. We loved being lukewarm. If the water had been too hot or too cold, we wouldn't have enjoyed it. But it was so pleasant that we returned often to be pampered. Here was a place where it was acceptable to be lazy. Sounds decadent, right? It was! We didn't go to Bad Ragaz to get revved up to take on new challenges. Just the opposite. We went there to wind down. It wasn't energizing; it was de-energizing. Afterward all we felt like doing was hurrying home to take a nap.

Unfortunately, what is wonderful in a spa is dreadful in a church. Anything that causes spiritual complacency—or, should I say, comfort—distracts us from one of Christianity's primary missions, which is attending to the needs of others. Why do we hesitate to help others? Do we fear being rejected or being accused of meddling? I doubt it. I've found that most of us avoid ministering to those in need not because we're afraid of failure, but because we're afraid of *success*. We're afraid God might be so pleased with our acts of service that He will call on us again...and again...and again...and again. We commit to God our time, talent, money, and energy, but at the same time fear that He may overwhelm us with more people in need. Oh dear, we don't want that! Can't we just engage in the occasional good deed and then relax? We don't want Christian duty to disrupt our spiritual spa time.

Because we are selfish by nature, we prefer a spiritual bask over a spiritual task. We like keeping our spiritual thermostats set at a comfortable temperature all the time. And we like the temperature in our churches to be the same. The moderate range is our comfort zone.

Let's admit it. It's easy to get addicted to moderation. Moderation feels good. Moderation is safe. Moderation reduces risk and allows us to maintain control. Why be a fired up, radical Christian when keeping our faith setting in the middle feels so good? Passionate faith is uncomfortable. That's why we avoid it.

Cold cash and a lukewarm spirit

A while back I was talking to a friend who had fallen out with his 82-year-old father, a man of considerable wealth. The old man's life had been spent pursuing his own ambitions and becoming financially comfortable. But one day he realized his pursuit of success had taken a toll on his family, so he gathered his wife and children and apologized. He then invited them to come to him in the future if they need help. A short time later, my friend suffered a series of financial setbacks and decided to take his father up on his offer. But his father refused his request. Instead he lectured his son on why it never works to loan money to family members or get involved in their affairs. "Go sort it out for yourself," the old man told his son. "It will be good for you."

My friend had had enough. After a lifetime of being shamed and rejected by his father, my friend realized his dad had issued a false promise. The paternal pledge was invalid as soon as the cost was too high. With hurt in his voice, my friend made this sad but profound observation, "My dad won't help anyone if it requires of him some measure of sacrifice." This prompted me to wonder if there is ever a time when helping someone doesn't cost us something. I can't think of any. Can you?

Unlike my friend's father, God doesn't make false promises or withhold help from His children. On the contrary, Malachi 3:6-7 reveals God's relentless generosity being extended even to those who reject Him. *"I the Lord do not change. So you, the descendants of Jacob, are not destroyed. Ever since the time of your ancestors you have turned away from my decrees and have not kept them. Return to me, and I will return to you," says the Lord Almighty.* God gives the rebellious Israelites—His chosen people—another chance to draw on His favor.

In Romans 8:28-30 (cited at the end of this chapter), Paul describes God's boundless offer of love and forgiveness. When it comes to our relationship with God, who chooses whom? Both Testaments declare that God chooses us, not vice versa. This goes against the popular notion that we initiate the divine-human relationship.

Based on what we're told in Malachi and Romans, God's choices are supreme and immutable. And once He has chosen us, we have no veto power. God does not vacillate, and His will is irresistible. *However*, Scripture also teaches that God grants us a certain amount of freedom (called limited freewill) in how we respond to being chosen. While God initiates our salvation, we are still free to decide whether or not to cooperate with His purposes. If we ignore God's invitation and go our own way, we turn our backs on His favor and enter into the chilly realm of self-rule. Rather than embracing God's supportive warmth, we choose to step back and keep our cool.

The author of Hebrews has more to say about spiritual temperature and temperament in Hebrews 3:12-13. *"See to it, brothers and sisters, that none of you has a sinful, unbelieving heart that turns away from the living God. But encourage one another daily, as long as it is called 'Today,' so that none of you may be hardened by sin's deceitfulness."* We must resist the urge to stray because turning away from God's light leaves us in darkness. And when that happens, the Holy Spirit withdraws. To ensure this doesn't happen, we're told to huddle together like children on a cold night and draw heat from one another. This is the power of spiritual companionship (or fellowship). Every soul in the circle is warmed by the others.

In 2 Peter 2:20-21, we find an unnerving description of the life of a spiritual stray. *"If they have escaped the corruption of the world by knowing our Lord and Savior Jesus Christ and are again entangled in it and are overcome, they are worse off at the end than they were at the beginning. It would have been better for them not to have known the way of righteousness, than to have known it and then to turn their backs on the sacred command that was passed on to them."* In Christian parlance, wandering away from God after having known Him is called "backsliding." This is worse than never knowing God at all. The person who has had no exposure to God's love and grace can plead ignorance. But what excuse is there for the one who *has* experienced God's loving favor and chooses to walk away? As we discussed earlier, it is enough to make the Lord sick to His stomach.

Fanning the flames of a flickering faith

One final point. We can't measure someone's body temperature without a physical touch. Likewise, we can't measure someone's spiritual temperature from a distance. Nor can we gauge the spiritual warmth of a congregation by merely watching them worship. I've attended churches where the worshipers are stoked with emotion, only to find out later that they lack maturity and depth. Their worship is hot, but their hearts are not. On the other hand, I've attended churches where worshipers are so restrained that they seem frozen, but on closer examination, I discovered that their hearts are warm and open, and they give sacrificially. Don't be fooled by outward appearances or trip over first impressions. Those are mistakes made by Pharisees.

Since judging others is not included in a Christian's job description, we acknowledge that *only* God is qualified to scrutinize the human heart or take a spiritual temperature. The one thing Scripture permits (and exhorts) us to do is monitor *our own* spiritual levels. When I sense a drop in my own spiritual temperature, I should take it as a warning sign: The flame of faith within me is flickering and needs to be fanned.

Hebrews 5:12-14 gives practical advice for how to revive a flickering fire of faith. More fuel is required. This passage presents yet another metaphor for reviving faith: It must be fed with "milk" for newcomers and "meat" for veterans. The author writes, *"In fact, though by this time you ought to be teachers, you need someone to teach you the elementary truths of God's word all over again. You need milk, not solid food! Anyone who lives on milk, being still an infant, is not acquainted with the teaching about righteousness. But solid food is for the mature, who by constant use have trained themselves to distinguish good from evil."* A physical body cannot retain heat without caloric fuel, and a spiritual body cannot retain warmth without a regular feeding on God's Word.

If you are feeling the spiritual chills presently, your diet may be lacking in the soul food of Scripture. Perhaps you have abandoned regular prayer and/or strayed from God's family circle. Many things can cause a drop in spiritual temperature, but ignoring the basic spiritual disciplines certainly accelerates the cool-down. We are warmed in God's presence, just as He is warmed in ours. As we draw closer to God and bask in His warmth, something else happens. The warmth of His Spirit is poured into us, and we share its warmth with the cooler souls around us. This is God's greater purpose: to draw us into warmer relationships, both vertically and horizontally. God's Spirit emanates through us to melt even the coldest hearts.

Satan, the master of mediocrity

As long as we live in this world, we will find ourselves in the heat of spiritual conflict. This is a controversial topic today, even in Christian circles. To some, using labels like "good" and "evil" is seen as bellicose language that sows discord. However, just because something causes discomfort doesn't mean it's wrong. I've found that uncomfortable truth is often the truth I most need to hear. There is a force in this world hell-bent on distracting us from our primary purpose, which is to live in harmony with our Creator and our fellow humans. But doing so means having to overcome a very real and formidable foe. He is Satan. And he is the preeminent destroyer of relationships.

Why are the mental and spiritual distractions around us so seductive? And why do they seem to be increasing exponentially? I believe it is because Satan is a genius at creating amusements and temptations to keep us from focusing on the sacred. And never has he had such a plethora of tools at his disposal. The electronic media and internet monopolize our attention to such an extent that we no longer take the time to think, study, pray, or ponder things eternal. This cacophony of artificial and superficial noise has made us deaf to the voice of God.

If your spiritual life has gone cold, don't expect it to warm up anytime soon. Satan is committed to keeping us lukewarm. Tepid. Comfortable. Mediocre. Complacent. Lazy. Sedated on self-satisfaction. As long as he keeps us hooked on the soul-numbing elixir of mediocrity, he has us where he wants us. Stuck in a spiritual stupor.

My advice? Don't drink the Kool-Aid. It will kill you! Instead, invite the Holy Spirit to fill you with the warmth of Christ to stave off the chills. There is no mediocre setting on the thermostats of those who love God passionately.

Additional readings

But if serving the Lord seems undesirable to you, then choose for yourselves this day whom you will serve, whether the gods your ancestors served beyond the Euphrates, or the gods of the Amorites, in whose land you are living. But as for me and my household, we will serve the Lord. — **Joshua 24:15**

Not everyone who says to me, 'Lord, Lord,' will enter the kingdom of heaven, but only the one who does the will of my Father who is in heaven. — **Matthew 7:21**

Therefore keep watch because you do not know when the owner of the house will come back — whether in the evening, or at midnight, or when the rooster crows, or at dawn. If he comes suddenly, do not let him find you sleeping. — **Mark 13:35-36**

And we know that in all things God works for the good of those who love him, who have been called according to his purpose. For those God foreknew he also predestined to be conformed to the image of his Son, that he might be the firstborn among many brothers and sisters. And those he predestined, he also called; those he called, he also justified; those he justified, he also glorified. — **Romans 8:28-30**

For the Spirit God gave us does not make us timid, but gives us power, love and self-discipline. — **2 Timothy 1:7**

But mark this: There will be terrible times in the last days. People will be lovers of themselves, lovers of money, boastful, proud, abusive, disobedient to their parents, ungrateful, unholy, without love, unforgiving, slanderous, without self-control, brutal, not lovers of the good, treacherous, rash, conceited, lovers of pleasure rather than lovers of God — having a form of godliness but denying its power. Have nothing to do with such people. — **2 Timothy 3:1-5**

Consider it pure joy, my brothers and sisters, whenever you face trials of many kinds, because you know that the testing of your faith produces perseverance. Let perseverance finish its work so that you may be mature and complete, not lacking anything. If any of you lacks wisdom, you should ask God, who gives generously to all without finding fault, and it will be given to you. But when you ask, you must believe and not doubt, because the one who doubts is like a wave of the sea, blown and tossed by the wind. That person should not expect to receive anything from the Lord. Such a person is double-minded and unstable in all they do. But when you ask, you must believe and not doubt, because the one who doubts is like a wave of the sea, blown and tossed by the wind. — **James 1:2-6**

Do not love the world or anything in the world. If anyone loves the world, love for the Father is not in them. For everything in the world — the lust of the flesh, the lust of the eyes, and the pride of life — comes not from the Father but from the world. — **1 John 2:15-16**

Chapter 15
TIME, WORRY AND REGRET

"I believe God is managing affairs and that He doesn't need any advice from me. With God in charge, I believe everything will work out for the best in the end. So what is there to worry about?" — **Henry Ford**

"Worry never robs tomorrow of its sorrow, it only saps today of its joy."
— **Leo Buscaglia**

"Worrying is praying to the wrong god." — **author unknown**

"Never look back unless you are planning to go that way."
— **Henry David Thoreau**

"Make it a rule of life never to regret and never to look back. Regret is an appalling waste of energy; you can't build on it; it's only good for wallowing in." — **Katherine Mansfield**

One of our greatest challenges in life is coming to terms with the passing of time. Put another way, we have a hard time accepting how brief our lives on earth really are. Our journey from the past to the future is over quickly, which is hard enough, but there also are so many obstacles along the way. Two of the biggest obstacles are worry and regret. They hang us up and cause us to miss out on the wonder of each precious moment that whizzes by. Worse yet, worry and regret throw our emotions off kilter and steal our joy.

Worry is allowing the uncertainty of the future to torment us. And regret is allowing the past we cannot change to do the same. Notice that the emotional dynamics are identical but focused in opposite directions. Regret is worry projected backward, and worry is regret projected forward. Sadly, both prevent us from having any peace in the present.

When we become ill, we treat the symptoms. But it's better to discover and eliminate what is causing our illness. I believe the primary component of both worry and regret is a refusal to accept the immutable nature of time and our inability to change it. Volumes have been written about these two emotional hazards, but my purpose here is to deal with their root cause: a flawed understanding of time.

Taking the fast train

Funny enough, I don't think I've ever heard a sermon on the nature of time. That may be because we clergy are too preoccupied and stressed out to ponder such things. Our sermons may seem to drone on forever, but like everyone else, we're just trying to cope moment by moment. Joking aside, I suspect there's a more serious reason why time isn't high on a preacher's list of favorite topics. Contemplating time and eternity is exhausting because it takes us into the fog of philosophy. One has only to read the renowned philosophers to know this. Socrates. Aristotle. Plato. Augustine. Kant. Hegel. Descartes. Rousseau. Nietzsche. Heidegger. Their names alone are daunting, but their ponderous writings are too much for most of us.

If the world's greatest minds can't explain the mysteries of time, perhaps a tale from the Wild West can get us started. In 1878, a Canadian railway engineer by the name of Sandford Fleming developed the system of worldwide time zones still used today. The advent of the railroad made such zoning necessary as people and goods began traveling greater distances at higher speeds. Fleming's time zones officially went into effect in the United States on November 18, 1883.

This modern innovation was particularly confusing for one old hermit living in the hills near the little town of Van Horn in West Texas. The man had a sister he hadn't seen in years, so he decided to leave his shack and take the train to visit her. She lived in Fort Hancock, just 50 miles west of Van Horn. He packed a bag, hiked the long distance into town, found the train station, and asked the ticket teller if there was a train running from Van Horn to Fort Hancock.

"Yessir," the ticket agent told him, "it leaves here at 10 o'clock."

"And what time does it get to Fort Hancock?" the old man asked.

"It arrives there at 10 o'clock, sir. Would you like to buy a ticket?"

The hermit said nothing, stepped away, and scratched his head. He knew nothing about the new time zone system. Nor did he realize that the dividing line for the new Central and Mountain Time Zones ran between Van Horn and Fort Hancock, a journey of exactly 60 minutes by rail.

After many minutes, the old man turned back to the ticket teller and said, "You say the train leaves here at 10 o'clock?"

"Yessir, that's right."

"And it arrives in Fort Hancock at 10 o'clock?"

"Yes, Mister, that's right," the teller replied impatiently. "Now do you want to buy a ticket for that train or don't you?"

"Naw," the old codger answered, "I don't think so. I'll just stick around and watch that sucker take off!"

This story serves to remind us how helpless we are when it comes to wrapping our minds around the complexities of time. And in spite of recent discoveries in the fields of astronomy, cosmology, and astrophysics, it seems that the more we know the more confounded we are. This much is clear: Time marches on, and it will continue to march on relentlessly with or without us.

The two leading time paradigms

As I said earlier, I believe the greatest cause of worry and regret is our flawed thinking about the nature of time and our inability to accept our place within it. When it comes to understanding the nature of time, there are two basic camps. The first is the **Eastern (or Oriental) View**, which describes time as cyclical, with no starting point, no transcendent purpose, and no ultimate culmination. The symbol that best captures the Eastern View is a circle. Round and around it goes, always returning to the same place and then starting over.

The second approach is the **Western (or Occidental) View**, which depicts time as linear, having started at some point before recorded history and moving toward a conclusion in the distant future. The symbol for the Western View is a horizontal line, usually shown as an arrow moving from left to right, from past to future.

We live in a world of three dimensions: length (or height), width (or breadth), and depth. Expanding our view beyond these categories requires taking the leap from science to science fiction. Mr. Einstein and his colleagues, along with many of our finest religionists and philosophers, have done their best to breach the vast chasm between the human realm and the multi-dimensional universe, but even our brightest minds don't possess the skills to fathom these mysteries or explain them in a way anyone can comprehend.

So where does this leave us? We are beings that spend the first half of our lives eagerly anticipating the future—and ambitiously charging into it—while at the same time trying to avoid thinking about the inevitability of our own death. Then, as we move into the latter part of our lives, we become preoccupied with our physical decline and start to dread our imminent departure. What strange creatures we are! We're perpetually torn between looking ahead and looking back, sensing that we are caught between this temporal world and the unknown realm of the eternal.

God in His wisdom has ordained that we live our early years in a state of blissful ignorance about what lies ahead. We should thank Him for that, for if He allowed us to gaze into the future, it's likely we would spend the rest of our days overwhelmed with fear about what is coming. Sadly, this describes many who suffer from certain psychological disorders. They live with mental torment, paranoia, and chronic anxiety, unable to bear not knowing and not having control.

Strangely enough, without a certain amount of ignorance, it is impossible to maintain health and balance in our lives. Just imagine how hellish your life would be if you knew everything all the time. How could you have hope? How could you dream dreams and plan plans? What kind of future would you prepare for your descendants? Unfortunately, we occasionally get a glimpse of such fatalism when we see older adults adopt a devil-may-care attitude and squander their assets in one final flurry of self-indulgence before they die. Irrespective of age, our beliefs about what will come tomorrow profoundly influence our actions today.

Thankfully, the Creator has made us just as we are. We have no design flaws. And, like it or not, God's design works. He allows us to know what has happened in the past but doesn't allow us to know what will happen in the future. If we knew ahead of time what's coming, we would never get out of bed. Our ignorance about the future is a blessing in disguise because it enables us to greet each day with anticipation and a measure of optimism. Knowing the details about the future would eliminate spontaneity and vibrancy from our lives. How good it is to be able to embark on a new adventure each and every morning! We should thank God for withholding from us information about the future. This is information with which we can't be trusted. Our attitude should always be, "Thank you for keeping me ignorant, God; I can't wait to see what happens next."

Paradox and the third paradigm

So here we are, stuck in time and space, trying to make the best of it. Whether we realize it or not, we are passengers on a train headed into the next time zone, and there's no getting off. Either we sit back and enjoy the ride, or we give in to fear and worry. For some of us, the prospect of roaring ahead into an uncertain future causes great stress. When that happens, damage control is required.

Earlier I presented the two pre-eminent paradigms for understanding the nature of time. You should know that there is a third: *The Biblical View* of time. Scripture blends together the Eastern and Western views of time to create a paradigm that is both cyclical *and* linear. The symbol that best captures this unique model is an uncoiling and expanding series of connected concentric rings:

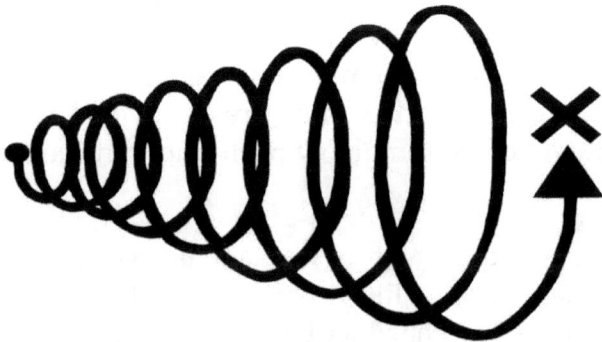

You'll notice that the connecting loops move from left to right, with each loop larger than the previous one. While there are similarities between the loops, their scale and breadth expand as they move from the beginning point to the end point, marked with an X.

To see how this works, apply it to the wars humankind has waged down through the centuries. These conflicts are never the same and their consequences differ in scale. Bows and arrows can be formidable weapons, but they are primitive compared to nuclear bombs. An army on horseback is nothing compared to a division of tanks. Storming a village is one thing, but wreaking destruction upon an entire continent is something else. With each new rotation of history, we sense having been here before, but we also sense something is different this time around. The scale of violence and devastation increases with each successive loop.

According to Scripture, time is a divine invention embedded in the fabric of creation. In Genesis 1:14-19, God forms the heavenly bodies (every element in the universe) and assigns to each a given space. However, it isn't until the *fourth* "day" that God sets this celestial array into motion. This marks the beginning of time, or what's been called "the cosmic clock." During the previous three "days," there was no animation (or motion). The essential element of time is animation. Here is the Bible's version of Einstein's fourth dimension. Time began at the moment everything started moving. Imagine what it was like to watch *that* sucker take off!

From Genesis 1:14 through the final "Amen" in Revelation 22:21, the Bible describes time as having cyclical elements and recurring similarities (see Ecclesiastes). But time never reverses itself or returns to the same place twice. Scriptural time is progressive, moving from a starting point to its culmination at the end of time. This is a paradox. Biblical time is cyclical, like the seasons, with no two seasons being exactly the same, but it also moves linearly, progressing from one point to the next and never static.

Our chronographs and calendars incorporate a mix of East and West. Some of our instruments record time in a circular mode, such as the hands on a clock, while others, such as calendars and timelines, measure time on a linear scale. These instruments are complementary and, as with any paradox, it isn't a matter of either/or; it is *both/and*. Hence, we have invented these various methods of recording time.

Every analysis of time reaches the same conclusion: We can do absolutely nothing to affect the passage of time. Wearing a watch may give us the illusion that we are "keeping time," but, in truth, *time keeps us.* As we come to accept the fact that in our dimension time moves in only one direction—from past to future and from one moment to the next—we must also accept our limitations. We are finite. We have been given only so much time and are subject to its laws. Stories about time travel fascinate us, but they are science fiction. Even the label science fiction is misleading; it is neither pure science nor pure fiction, but a combination of both. While experiments using atomic clocks have given credence to Albert Einstein's Theory of Relativity, the mysteries of time continue to confound us. We may be able to fantasize about venturing into the fourth dimension, but the ability to actually do so eludes us. God's sovereignty in these matters is unthreatened. All we can do is exist at the mercy of time.

Fools, cocoons, and eggshells

The Book of Job addresses our age-old longing to understand life's deepest mysteries. The greater portion of the narrative is devoted to the ruminations of Job and his friends about God's purposes and humanity's part in them. Chapter after chapter, these blind guides banter, until finally, in the 38th chapter, God silences them by asking, "Who do you think you are?" He admonishes them for judging the Almighty. How dare they utter words so devoid of knowledge and wisdom! Once God becomes the interrogator, the tables turn. He challenges Job to explain the dynamics of light and darkness, how the planets function and the elements respond, and how the universe and natural events are scheduled. God's questions assault Job's feeble intellect, causing him to fall to the ground and beg for mercy. Job suddenly realizes how foolish he has been in speaking about *"things too wonderful for [him] to know."* (Job 42:1-3) Job and his would-be counselors had dared to enter the forbidden arena of divine mystery, and their ignorance had been exposed.

Don't we do the same when we ask questions with answers our minds can't handle? Like Job and his friends, we grope about in ignorance and stumble on our own vanity and pride. We are short on wisdom and long on folly, producing only hot air. We are so intellectually stunted that when it comes to trying to understand the things of God, we find that we are in way over our heads.

Of the four gospel writers, John dwells the most on the mysteries of time. Not only was he a brilliant theologian, he was also a philosopher, his writings showing an understanding of Hellenism (his Greek/Western context) as well as a solid grasp of his Jewish (Eastern/Oriental) roots. In the first chapter of his gospel—and in all the documents traditionally ascribed to him: the three Epistles of John and the Book of Revelation—John pushes us beyond our finite perceptions and gives us glimpses into infinity. He scans the spectrum of time and sees beyond the traditional categories. He envisions a multi-dimensional reflection of time as created by God. In other words, John sees the BIG picture and describes it for the rest of us. It is a remarkable disclosure.

John isn't the only biblical author who contemplates the nature of time. The Book of Psalms is laden with references to the eternal realm, eloquently describing life beyond the worldly veil. Psalm 23:6 makes the promise that those who are loved by God will *"dwell in the house of the Lord forever."* Psalm 37:18 says that the Lord holds our earthly lives in His hands and bestows upon us an *"inheritance [that] will endure forever."* Virtually every poem in the Psalter, either directly or indirectly, links the temporal realm to the eternal, with one overlapping the other.

Then there's the Apostle Paul. His reflections on the nature of time are equally compelling. *"When the perishable has been clothed with the imperishable, and the mortal with immortality, then the saying that is written will come true: 'Death has been swallowed up in victory.' 'Where, O death, is your victory? Where, O death, is your sting?"* (1 Cor. 15:54-55; Isaiah 25:8; Hosea 13:14) Once our souls enter the eternal realm, our physical bodies are no longer needed.

Simon Peter's description of the next world confirms Paul's. He refers to our bodies as "tents," presently occupied but soon to be abandoned. (See 2 Cor. 5:1 and 2 Peter 1:13-14.)

These tents are accommodating at the moment, but eventually they will dry out, become threadbare, and can no longer contain our spirits. Then our eternal essence will depart, leaving behind an empty container like the vacated cocoon of a butterfly or the shell of an empty egg.

Stripping away illusions

The thought of making the transition from this world to the next may frighten you. But hang in there. God has a way of preparing us for our inevitable departure. I have found that one positive aspect of aging—and there aren't many—is that it slowly and methodically removes my long-held illusions and prepares me for the final letting go of this world. And as this happens, my physical resources diminish, making my eventual spiritual release more welcome. I'll give you an example. In my younger days, I enjoyed playing basketball. I could easily jump up and grab the rim, block shots, and run the court for hours. But one day I discovered that I could no longer reach the rim. A few years later, I could barely touch the bottom of the net. My vertical game had disappeared, forcing me to come to terms with the harsh reality that I could no longer keep up with the younger guys. Ouch. Now, decades on, I find that any dribbling I do isn't with a basketball. However, I've come to see that this is just one of the many dents age is making on my body. Only by experiencing these physical regressions do I begin to accept that this is nature's way of slowing me down and stripping away my illusions of eternal youthfulness. I have gradually come to see that God is preparing me for what comes next, and that is as it should be.

As a minister, my profession allows me the privilege of being present with people when they are in the process of dying. These experiences have strengthened my conviction that our primary residence is not here on earth. Since our truest nature is spiritual, our actual home is in eternity. We are only temporary visitors here on earth. If you think this life is all there is, and this is as good as it gets, I suggest you try something. The next time you walk past a cemetery pause to gaze upon the tombstones. Who were those people? And where are they now? Who remembers them? How long did they live? What were their final thoughts before they abandoned their tents? You will never know. But now consider—and I don't mean this to sound morbid—that you will be joining them sooner than you think. What thoughts will fill *your* head just before you close your eyes on that final day? And what will you expect to see when you open your immortal eyes on the other side? God only knows. But it's coming. And it's coming fast! That is the plain, undeniable truth.

So, what's it all about?

In 1 John 5:11-12, we are given a critical insight into how one makes the transition from here to eternity: *"And this is the testimony: God has given us eternal life, and this life is in his Son. Whoever has the Son has life; whoever does not have the Son of God does not have life."* In the next verse, the author explains his purpose by sharing this: *"I write these things to you who believe in the name of the Son of God so that you may know that you have eternal life."* Why were John and his New Testament peers preoccupied with eternity? First, it's because this is the destiny God has promised and planned for every one of us. And second, it's because He wants us to know that how we live in this world will impact the quality of our existence in the next world. If there is nothing beyond this life and no consequences for how we live here, there are no grounds for hope and no basis for living a moral life. If this is all there is, life is cruel and absurd. In fact, it's utterly meaningless.

How do we decide what we should be doing on this side of eternity? Some of us devote ourselves to accumulating "stuff" and reveling in it, living as though "the one who dies with the most toys wins." Looking for meaning in acquisition and accumulation is understandable in a material world, but what might cause us to abandon our materialistic pursuits and seek greater meaning elsewhere? And does this mean dispensing of our worldly pleasures in hopes of finding something better on the other side?

Think of it this way. Much of our food today comes in cheap containers and is consumed using plastic utensils. Needless to say, we don't handle these disposable items the same way we handle grandmother's fine china and silver place settings. Why? Because the value we place on "things" is in direct proportion to the value we place on the people who provide those things for us. We should keep this in mind when we evaluate any investment we make. Our attitude toward money and possessions—and how we spend our time and energy—are indicators of who and what we love and respect. Our external investments reveal our internal values. If we love and respect God, we love and respect whatever belongs to Him. If we love and respect material wealth, we...well, you know the rest of the sentence.

Some men once tried to trap Jesus by questioning his economic and political loyalties. He answered by holding up a coin and saying, *"Give back to Caesar what is Caesar's and to God what is God's."* (Mark 12:17) Jesus cunningly tosses the coin aside and turns the question on them. What do they value the most? In doing so, he exposes not only his inquisitors' primary allegiances but also our own. Which master do we serve?

Rather than chasing after wealth and using it as leverage for self-gain, shouldn't I be invested in things that matter more? One surefire way of knowing the contents of my heart is by examining my bank accounts and personal schedule. How do I spend my money and time? Therein will my priorities be found. If I profess faith in Jesus Christ but there is no tangible evidence to support my profession, there is something wrong.

Taking it one step further, the things we value most are connected to the *people* we value most. If a beloved relative gives us a special gift, that gift will be cherished for its emotional value rather than its monetary value. The same applies to our connection to our heavenly Father. The more we cherish our relationship with God, the more we cherish His gifts, for they reflect His generosity to us.

As God's children, we must not treat His bountiful gifts to us like used paper cups or plastic forks. If creation, in all its aspects, is the handiwork of our Creator and provided for our enjoyment, how we handle every part of that creation should be a no-brainer.

So, what is the bottom line?

Life is all about relationships. It's about past, present, and future relationships. This is the central theme of Scripture and the ultimate meaning of life. Take away personal relationships and life becomes meaningless and absurd. But if we engage in nurturing relationships with God and those around us, life becomes rich, meaningful, and fulfilling. Life is all about relationships, vertical and horizontal.

Living between the "then" and the "when"

Let's get back to considering how we spend our time here in our earthly tents. Even though our essence is eternal, the only time that's available to us is the *right now*. We may remember the past, but we can't relive it or bring it into the here and now. The same is true of the future; it is inaccessible to us. We cannot project ourselves forward or bring parts of the future back into the present. As Emily Dickinson said so succinctly, "Forever—is composed of Nows." Even the comedian/philosopher Woody Allen, in his quirky way, makes this telling observation: "Eternity is really long, especially near the end." I'm not sure exactly what Allen meant, but I do believe he's onto something. Eternity is a *really* long time. And we are not there yet. However, God *is* there already, and He always has been. Just not in the way we may think.

I used to imagine that dying means leaving this dimension and moving into another dimension where time doesn't exist. But having recently read a message by a man named Jason Dulle, I'm reconsidering. I know nothing about Mr. Dulle, but I think he handles the mysteries of time and eternity in a way that is consistent with Scripture. I even appreciate his approach to the unwieldy topic of predestination. He makes sense. Dulle says this:

> Eternity is not timelessness per se, but is never-ending time. Time will be irrelevant in eternity. We will not measure time, and therefore will not be conscious of its passing, but nevertheless it will still exist. We use the sun, stars, and moon to measure the passing of time in our present world. With such, we come up with ideas such as hours, days, weeks, months, years and so on. In eternity there will be no cosmos to measure time. There will be no night because Jesus will light the New Jerusalem (Revelation 21:23-26). ...Time is a creation by God, which is necessary for the existence of the created reality. Present time is the only time that truly exists. The past and future are only perspectives of time from the mind of the knower. Though the past is real, in that it *did* happen, and the future will be real, in that it *will* happen, the only time that exists is the present. This understanding of time leads us to believe that eternity will not be timelessness but will be never-ending time. It also leads us to believe that the out-workings of our lives are of the utmost importance to God, and that His foreknowledge of the future does not make human action meaningless or unnecessary.[28]

Victims *of* time or victors *over* time?

Biblical theology makes room for plenty of philosophical speculation, but it doesn't allow for fatalism, which is the belief that nothing we do in this life matters because it's all left to "fate." I don't think the God of Scripture has programmed the future and made us automatons to play out His pre-written script. We have been given an independent will. We are not helpless. God has empowered us to be active participants in our own destiny,

---

[28] http://www.onenesspentecostal.com/time.htm

perhaps not in the sense that we direct the action, but by allowing us to choose whether or not to cooperate with His plans as the real director. More importantly, God has chosen to be just as active in the "here and now" as He is in the eternal realm, although the details of His involvement remain mysterious.

Thanks to God's revelation in Jesus Christ, one thing we can know for sure is that God has invited us to maintain our relationship with Him in the next life. Jesus is the only person who has commuted between the temporal and eternal realms, and he spoke these assuring words: *"My sheep listen to my voice; I know them, and they follow me. I give them eternal life, and they shall never perish; no one will snatch them out of my hand."* (John 10:27-28) Having been raised as a churchgoer, I heard these two verses read many times. But it wasn't until I was 20 that they started to sink in. Since then, Christ's assuring words have become more comforting and enticing for me with each passing year.

The Bible's promises have sustained me throughout my life-journey and heightened my anticipation about what's ahead. Knowing that God has watched over me in the past, continues to protect me in the present, and has arranged for my future in eternity is all I need. This knowledge helps to dispel my regrets and lessen my anxieties. God has gotten me this far, so I'm trusting Him to get me the rest of the way. Best of all, the next leg of this exciting journey will be eternal.

I look forward to watching that train take off. Because I will be on it!

Additional readings

There is a time for everything, and a season for every activity under the heavens: a time to be born and a time to die, a time to plant and a time to uproot, a time to kill and a time to heal, a time to tear down and a time to build, a time to weep and a time to laugh, a time to mourn and a time to dance, a time to scatter stones and a time to gather them, a time to embrace and a time to refrain from embracing, a time to search and a time to give up, a time to keep and a time to throw away, a time to tear and a time to mend, a time to be silent and a time to speak, a time to love and a time to hate, a time for war and a time for peace.

What do workers gain from their toil? I have seen the burden God has laid on the human race. He has made everything beautiful in its time. He has also set eternity in the human heart; yet no one can fathom what God has done from beginning to end. I know that there is nothing better for people than to be happy and to do good while they live. That each of them may eat and drink, and find satisfaction in all their toil — this is the gift of God. I know that everything God does will endure forever; nothing can be added to it and nothing taken from it. God does it so that people will fear him. Whatever is has already been, and what will be has been before; and God will call the past to account.

— Ecclesiastes 3:1-15

"For I know the plans I have for you," declares the Lord, "plans to prosper you and not to harm you, plans to give you hope and a future."

— Jeremiah 29:11

Therefore I tell you, do not worry about your life, what you will eat or drink; or about your body, what you will wear. Is not life more than food, and the body more than clothes? Look at the birds of the air; they do not sow or reap or store away in barns, and yet your heavenly Father feeds them. Are you not much more valuable than they? Can any one of you by worrying add a single hour to your life? And why do you worry about clothes? See how the flowers of the field grow. They do not labor or spin. Yet I tell you that not even Solomon in all his splendor was dressed like one of these. If that is how God clothes the grass of the field, which is here today and tomorrow is thrown into the fire, will he not much more clothe you — you of little faith? So do not worry, saying, 'What shall we eat?' or 'What shall we drink?' or 'What shall we wear?' For the pagans run after all these things, and your heavenly Father knows that you need them. But seek first his kingdom and his righteousness, and all these things will be given to you as well. Therefore do not worry about tomorrow, for tomorrow will worry about itself. Each day has enough trouble of its own. **— Matthew 6:25-34**

Now listen, you who say, "Today or tomorrow we will go to this or that city, spend a year there, carry on business and make money." Why, you do not even know what will happen tomorrow. What is your life? You are a mist that appears for a little while and then vanishes. Instead, you ought to say, "If it is the Lord's will, we will live and do this or that." — **James 4:13-15**

But do not forget this one thing, dear friends: With the Lord a day is like a thousand years, and a thousand years are like a day. The Lord is not slow in keeping his promise, as some understand slowness. Instead he is patient with you, not wanting anyone to perish, but everyone to come to repentance. — **2 Peter 3:8-9**

Chapter 16

YOU GOTTA SERVE SOMEBODY

"Obedience to lawful authority is the foundation of manly character."
— Robert E. Lee

"You are what you do, not what you say you'll do."
— Carl Gustav Jung

"The fruit of Love is service. The fruit of Service is peace."
— Mother Teresa

"I don't know what your destiny will be, but one thing I know: the only ones among you who will be really happy are those who have sought and found how to serve." — **Albert Schweitzer**

"Relationships are never about power, and one way to avoid the will to power is to choose to limit oneself – to serve." — **William Paul Young**

"No one can serve two masters. Either you will hate the one and love the other, or you will be devoted to the one and despise the other. You cannot serve both God and money." — **Matthew 6:24**

In 1979, a poet/musician from Hibbing, Minnesota by the name of Bobby Zimmerman composed a song about the vocational, social, and lifestyle decisions people make in life. After listing the many options, Zimmerman reached the conclusion that drives the song's chorus:

> *But you're gonna have to serve somebody, yes indeed,*
> *You're gonna have to serve somebody.*
> *Well, it may be the devil or it may be the Lord,*
> *But you're gonna have to serve somebody.*

Of course, Mr. Zimmerman is better known by his stage name, Bob Dylan, and his song "Gotta Serve Somebody" has its place in his impressive catalog of hits. You will find the song's lyrics attached to the end of this chapter. They are worth contemplating.

Dylan has had such influence as a minstrel and cultural icon that he is recognized as a spokesman for America's post-WW2 generation. Like many of his peers, Dylan spent his life searching for meaning, trying everything from money to fame to sex to drugs to...whatever else tickled his fancy. After finding no fulfillment in any of these, Dylan turned his attention to the spiritual realm and experimented with atheism, cynicism, agnosticism, mysticism, and even Christianity before finally returning to his ethnic/religious roots of Judaism, which, I believe, is the faith he professes and practices today.

During the late 1970s, Dylan connected with the Christian community and began a serious study of the teachings of Jesus. As is his way, he shared his discoveries in song. In the lyrics of "Gotta Serve Somebody," Dylan declares that regardless of who we are or what we accomplish, in the end, we all have to serve *something* or *somebody*. We are never totally free, never fully self-sufficient. The Bible inspired Dylan's thesis. Or perhaps I should say Dylan confirms the Bible's thesis. Either way, the bottom line is the same: We all gotta serve somebody.

From a Judeo-Christian perspective, the key to improving our human conditions is embedded in Scripture. More specifically, it's found in passages like these:

Joshua 22:5: *Be very careful to keep the commandment and the law that Moses the servant of the Lord gave you: to love the Lord your God, to walk in obedience to him, to keep his commands, to hold fast to him and to serve him with all your heart and with all your soul.*

Deuteronomy 13:4: *It is the Lord your God you must follow, and him you must revere. Keep his commands and obey him; serve him and hold fast to him.*

Matthew 6:24: *No one can serve two masters. Either you will hate the one and love the other, or you will be devoted to the one and despise the other. You cannot serve both God and money.*

The verses above are in line with Dylan's assertion that freedom comes in choosing the right master to serve. The main factors that determine how we live our lives are found in the things our hearts crave and our minds focus on. In other words, our appetites and beliefs impact our choices. We pursue the things we want most, even to the point of enslavement. Either we refuse to resist the pull of temptation, or we surrender our will to other forces. And either way, we all end up serving a master of some kind, willingly or by default.

Choosing the wrong master

Scripture is full of people whose lives came unraveled after choosing the wrong master. First among them were Adam and Eve. Since they made their tragic choice, every one of us has had to follow suit and grapple with making our own choices. In the Book of Exodus, an Egyptian pharaoh made choices that unleashed the earthshaking events that followed — events that continue to rock our world today. Every ruler since has done likewise, deciding to serve one power over another and then dealing with the consequences. God sent prophets to warn these leaders to repent and submit to divine authority. But most of them refused and paid dearly for it. So did their subjects. Nebuchadnezzar. Ahab. Jezebel. Absalom. Herod. Pontius Pilate. The Bible's list of stubborn leaders who made disastrous choices is long and tragic. Virtually all of them chose the wrong "somebody" to serve.

Of course, kings and queens aren't the only ones who choose badly. In Matthew 19:16-22, a learned and affluent man comes to Jesus seeking the key to eternal life. Jesus tells him, *"Sell your possessions and give to the poor...then come, follow me."* This price was too high for the young man. He lowered his head, turned and walked away, shackled by his wealth.

The religious leaders of Jesus' day were enslaved in other ways. They were chained to their religious laws and addicted to control, caught up in legalism of their own making.

An even more sobering example of ill-advised servitude is found in Luke's gospel (23:39-43). Here we are told of the fateful choices made by the two criminals who died on the crosses flanking the crucified Christ. One accepts the lordship of Jesus and receives life; the other spurns Jesus and descends into oblivion. Nowhere do we see the consequences of our decisions more vividly than here.

Why do so many begin life with good intentions—and with so much potential—only to squander their lives on bad decisions? What could be more tragic than rejecting our higher calling in order to serve lesser gods? What causes our decision-making mechanism to short-circuit?

Serving the master Master

A better question may be: If God is the perfect Master, why don't we all serve Him? Perhaps we misunderstand what serving him requires of us. Does it mean going through life as good little girls and boys striving to impress Him and prove we're worthy of His favor? Is God a Master who demands that we surrender our own identity by submitting to His dictatorship? If that's how it works, Christianity is like being on a chain gang and living as convicted criminals. Is God a slave driver who cracks His whip and revels in watching us jump? If so, either we've gotten our theological wires crossed, or He can't be a Master worth serving.

As Bob Dylan contemplates which power to serve, he sings a song worthy of the Jewish minstrels that preceded him by a few thousand years. Ancient Israel's psalmists and sages had a passionate desire to know the nature of God, and they expressed their longings in song. Psalm 100 is a prime example. It's downright Dylanesque:

"Shout for joy to the Lord, all the earth. Worship the Lord with gladness; come before him with joyful songs. ...Enter his gates with

thanksgiving and his courts with praise; give thanks to him and praise his name. For the Lord is good and his love endures forever; his faithfulness continues through all generations."

This is more than the lament of a galley slave or the plea of an underling. These are lyrics written by a worldly ruler longing to serve in the court of the ultimate monarch. The composer—whom we believe was King David himself—knew that living in submission to the perfect king was better than having his own throne.

Dylan asks us to take seriously the question of whom we will serve. His lyrics betray that he knows there is one master who stands above all others. And that is *The Master*. Serving this Master is an honor. This Master rewards devotion with protection and provides for His servants' every need. Serving this Master is liberating. More amazing yet, this Master gives His servants access to His royal treasury and prepares a place for each of them at His banquet table. What sort of Master *is* this?

Subjection as liberation

For nearly 50 years, I have proudly worn a wedding ring on my left hand as a sign that I have chosen Susan to be my one-and-only. That thin, gold band declares my freedom. This is another paradox. In being bound to the one, I am free from all others. Knowing to whom I belong is liberating.

I wince whenever I hear someone compare marriage to slavery or refer to a spouse as a "ball and chain." This reduces matrimony to oppressive bondage rather than mutual submission in love as God designed it. My wedding ring is a public declaration of my intimate relationship with only one woman. I have never set foot in a singles bar, but if I were to do so, I would be the freest person in the room. Why? Because I don't belong there. I belong to Susan, and that makes me a *double* rather than a single. No matter where I am, I can engage with anyone or everyone in a safe, healthy way. No temptations. No hidden motives. No strings attached. Knowing who owns my heart gives me clarity and security. It is the person who doesn't belong to anyone that is most at risk.

This same principle applies whenever we find ourselves surrounded by forces vying to own us, striving to seduce us, or trying to enslave us. Some of these forces are overt. Others are covert. But their objective is the same: to lay claim over our mind, body, and soul.

Knowing our Master's will...and doing it

One of my favorite Christian authors is Gerald Sittser. His writings connect God's Word to life in the real world. In his book *The Will of God as a Way of Life,*[29] Sittser explains how we can know God's will and then apply ourselves to fulfilling it. He gives **six signs** to look for when trying to discern God's will:

First, we should look deep within ourselves to examine our motivations. What turns us on and fires us up? Once we have answered that question, we're well on our way to understanding what God has placed us here to do. When we discover what we love and then do it, we find that our passions align with God's purpose for us. God loves it when we love doing what He created us to do.

Second, we should take inventory of our God-given talents. Having a passion for something is one thing but possessing the skills to do it well is something else. If you love to sing but have a terrible voice, I'm sorry, but it's unlikely that God will be glorified when you sing in public. And no one else will enjoy it either! To fulfill our divine calling, we must possess the tools to do the job well.

Third, we must consider our life experiences. We often find that the happenstances of our lives direct us to something higher. How true this has been in my own life! I can look back and see so many things in my life—most of them unplanned and

---

[29] *The Will of God as a Way of Life: How to Make Every Decision with Peace and Confidence* by Gerald Sittser, Zondervan, Grand Rapids, Michigan, 2004. Formerly titled *Discovering God's Will* (2000). Pages cited 175-185.

unexpected—that have equipped me for a career in ministry. Each time I ponder what God might have for me next, my anxiety fades as I remember what He has done for me and through me in the past. God is the ultimate Manager. He enriches His servants' lives and then enriches the lives of others through them. In this way, He expands and strengthens His kingdom on earth to the benefit of all.

Fourth, we should know that a divine call brings with it a wealth of opportunities. And they will pop up at any moment to reveal God's will to us. There's no such thing as an accident or coincidence in God's scheme of things. *Everything* has a purpose. If a door opens, we had best pay attention. And if a door closes, we should be prepared to slam on the brakes and move in another direction.

Fifth, our calling becomes clearer as we become more actively involved in a community of faith. The voices of those who know and love us amplify the voice of God. Persons who share our vision and values help to steer us in the right direction and keep us from going astray. If I'm sensing that something in my life needs to change, I immediately sit down with trusted friends and family to share what I'm thinking and feeling. I then listen to what they have to say, allowing them to influence my decision. This process has saved me from making some bad moves. We may think we're doing God's will, but what if we're wrong? To reduce the odds of that happening, we must listen to the caring voices around us. God uses these voices to speak truth into our lives.

And **sixth**, God's call on our lives brings with it joy. Sittser defuses the assumption that doing God's will means having to bear heavy burdens. Believing that serving God brings misery makes us hesitant to enter into something good for fear that it will end up being bad for us. Does this make sense? Why would a loving God call us to do the very things we hate? If this is His way, God is like an employer who builds a business by forcing his employees to perform tasks they detest. In the short term, the work might get done, but in the long run, morale will tank and productivity will decline. For any organization to flourish, the benefits must outweigh the burdens, and there must be joy and mutual fulfillment in the endeavor.

While it's true that those who do God's bidding are not always happy, their basic disposition is joyful rather than woeful and gracious rather than grumbling. No parent enjoys sending his or her child into a miserable situation. Neither does God. He desires that we have fun and find pleasure in serving Him. God knows that we are healthier and happier when we enjoy what we are doing. His ideal is to empower us to live in such a way that our passions align with His purposes.

Mr. Dylan said we all "gotta serve somebody." Jesus puts it this way: *"No one can serve two masters."* So, who is *your* master? Whom do *you* serve? And does your service glorify Him or vilify Him? If you love God, you will serve Him and Him alone. Best of all, when you do this, you will find that serving Him gives your life meaning and contentment. Everybody wins.

"Gotta Serve Somebody"

You may be an ambassador to England or France,
You may like to gamble, you might like to dance,
You may be the heavyweight champion of the world,
You may be a socialite with a long string of pearls.

Chorus:
But you're gonna have to serve somebody,
Yes indeed, you're gonna have to serve somebody.
Well, it may be the devil or it may be the Lord,
But you're gonna have to serve somebody.

You might be a rock 'n' roll addict prancing on the stage,
You might have drugs at your command, women in a
cage, You may be a businessman or some high degree
thief, They may call you Doctor or they may call you
Chief.

You may be a state trooper, you might be a young Turk,

224

You may be the head of some big TV network, You may
be rich or poor, you may be blind or lame, You may be
living in another country under another name.

You may be a construction worker working on a home,
You may be living in a mansion or you might live in a
dome, You might own guns and you might even own
tanks, You might be somebody's landlord, you might
even own banks.

You may be a preacher with your spiritual pride,
You may be a city councilman taking bribes on the side,
You may be workin' in a barbershop, you may know
how to cut hair; You may be somebody's mistress, may
be somebody's heir.

Might like to wear cotton, might like to wear silk,
Might like to drink whiskey, might like to drink milk,
You might like to eat caviar, you might like to eat bread,
You may be sleeping on the floor, sleeping in a king-
sized bed.

You may call me Terry, you may call me Timmy,
You may call me Bobby, you may call me Zimmy,
You may call me R.J., you may call me Ray,
You may call me anything but no matter what you say.

You're gonna have to serve somebody,
Yes indeed, you're gonna have to serve somebody.
Well, it may be the devil or it may be the Lord,
But you're gonna have to serve somebody.

©1979, Music and Lyrics by Bob Dylan, from the album
Slow Train Coming.

Additional readings

But if serving the Lord seems undesirable to you, then choose for yourselves this day whom you will serve, whether the gods your ancestors served beyond the Euphrates, or the gods of the Amorites, in whose land you are living. But as for me and my household, we will serve the Lord. — **Joshua 24:15**

"On the day when I act," says the Lord Almighty, "they will be my treasured possession. I will spare them, just as a father has compassion and spares his son who serves him. And you will again see the distinction between the righteous and the wicked, between those who serve God and those who do not." — **Malachi 3:17-18**

But store up for yourselves treasures in heaven, where moths and vermin do not destroy, and where thieves do not break in and steal. For where your treasure is, there your heart will be also.

The eye is the lamp of the body. If your eyes are healthy, your whole body will be full of light. But if your eyes are unhealthy, your whole body will be full of darkness. If then the light within you is darkness, how great is that darkness!

No one can serve two masters. Either you will hate the one and love the other, or you will be devoted to the one and despise the other. You cannot serve both God and money. — **Matthew 6:20-24**

Whatever you do, work at it with all your heart, as working for the Lord, not for human masters, since you know that you will receive an inheritance from the Lord as a reward. It is the Lord Christ you are serving. — **Colossians 3:23-24**

Religion that God our Father accepts as pure and faultless is this: to look after orphans and widows in their distress and to keep oneself from being polluted by the world. — **James 1:27**

EPILOGUE

In my prologue, I stated my opinion that we are living in an era of hysteria where coping with our outer world is causing us to lose control of our inner world. I developed that thesis in the chapters that followed. Now I find myself at the end of the book. How can I wrap this up? Assuming that the current hysteria will not subside — and will probably increase — what hope and help can I leave with you? First, beware of those who allow their feelings to drown out the facts. Their voices are loud and seductive. Don't believe them. Facts should always hold sway over feelings. Second, trust your intuition and never lose your common sense. Fear is rampant today. And fear is a breeding ground for exploitation. Protect your mind and heart from the exploiters. They feast on your feelings. Stay focused on the bigger truths and you won't get hung up on little lies. God is still in control...and always has been.

While I try to avoid predicting what tomorrow may bring, the changes I've seen in my lifetime — along with the increasing volatility in our world — make it harder than ever to resist such speculation. Public polls, statistical analyses, and comparative studies support the same conclusion: We are engulfed in a riptide of rapid change from which there seems to be no escape.[30] What does this suggest about where we are headed? It sounds quite foreboding to me.

When anything, good or bad, is doubled repeatedly (exponentially) over a period of time, eventually a point is reached where the growth curve collapses. Our world is caught up in a wave of exponential growth, and many are sensing that the point of collapse is just around the corner. Our natural resources are rapidly being depleted. Climatic change is afoot. Population figures are mounting. Technology is threatening our

---

[30] Exponential (adjective): 1. of or relating to an exponent or exponents; 2. *Mathematics:* of or relating to the constant e. (of an equation) having one or more unknown variables in one or more exponents.

humanity. This is our predicament. Nothing in the natural realm can continue growing ad infinitum. Something's gotta give.

How can we live with so much stress? And how can we maintain emotional health in a world where the line between what is real and what is not is so sketchy? To muddle things further, most of the residents of our planet now have access to cyberspace, which has us treading water in a churning sea of information without "truth preservers." No previous generation has been so swamped with truth-claims and subjective realities, all of them competing for our attention and vying for our trust. It's hard to stay afloat in waters that are rising so fast and furious.

Regardless of whether or not we apply the exponential equation to population growth, the economy, petroleum reserves, acres of arable land, food supplies, or anything else, there is no denying that the world as we know it will not last forever. Sooner or later, we will lose the numbers game. We are reaching the end of our rope. If you think I'm overstating this, consider the list of priorities announced recently by NASA and other space agencies.[31] The list reveals that the scientific community knows our days on earth are numbered, and unless some unforeseen event changes our current course — or we find another planet to accommodate us — our goose is cooked.

Over 2,500 years ago, the Old Testament prophet Daniel was given a glimpse of the conditions on earth just before the culmination of history, a time that Scripture speaks of often but never fully unveils. In the Book of Daniel, chapter 12, verse 4, we read: *"But you, Daniel, roll up and seal the words of the scroll until the time of the end. Many will go here and there to increase knowledge."* What I find remarkable about this text is how *unremarkable* it is. Here is the punchline of Daniel's prophecy: He describes the scenario on earth during the final days as a time when *"many will [be going] here and there to increase knowledge."* Wham!

---

[31] http://rt.com/news/mars-human-ultimate-destination-nasa-904/

"Okay," you may say, "Is that it? Is there really something significant in this vague description?" I believe there is. As is always the case with Scripture, there's more here than meets the eye. If this verse is a description of our global society immediately before the closure of time, what is it telling us? It appears to me that two outstanding factors will be evident in those final days. First, people will have access to unlimited travel ("going here and there"). And, second, people will have an insatiable appetite for — and access to — boundless information ("increasing knowledge"). Does this ring any bells for you?

I admit that trying to interpret the Bible's apocalyptic texts is a dodgy endeavor, but I find in Daniel's vision a fitting description of our world today. Unlimited global travel. Access to countless resources on the internet and World Wide Web. Twenty-first century technology has provided us with unprecedented ways to indulge our lust for adventure and our insatiable appetite for knowledge. Could it be that Daniel was given a glimpse into a future that is now upon us? And, if so, has he provided us with a preview of — and warning about — what God has in store for our planet?

For the sake of my argument, let's assume there is something in Daniel's vision that matches our present situation. So what? How does believing this ancient prophecy is being fulfilled before our eyes change anything? How does it impact our faith or influence our daily decisions and behavior? I believe the prophet's vision is not only relevant but essential for those who cling to *faith* in the midst of doubt, *hope* in the midst of hopelessness, and *love* in the midst of cynicism. Do these three platitudes sound familiar? They should. Read on.

If you look into the New Testament epistles, you'll find edification and enlightenment regarding these matters. Chapter 13 of Paul's first letter to the Corinthian Christians is recognized as one of the finest examples of prose in all of literature. It is Paul's famous "Love Chapter." Within its beautiful prose is a revelation that many readers miss. I have preached on this passage countless times, written commentaries on it, and included it in most of the weddings I've performed. And yet, it has taken me decades to discover the profound truth embedded in this text. Its essence is found in the closing crescendo, verses 12 and 13:

> For now we see only a reflection as in a mirror; then we shall see face to face. Now I know in part; then I shall know fully, even as I am fully known. And now these three remain: faith, hope and love. But the greatest of these is love.

If the New Testament's most prolific author and articulate theologian distilled his spiritual insights into one sweet morsel, we should take note. According to Paul, when all is said and done, there are **three truths** (or values) in the universe that stand above all others. They are: *faith, hope, and love,* three words that roll off the tongue but stagger the intellect. Paul has given us a capsulated theophany.

Several years ago, I was reading 1 Corinthians 13 for the umpteenth time and suddenly saw in the final two verses something I had missed. I went back and read those verses over and over again and asked myself, "Why faith, hope, and love? Why elevate these three virtues above all others? And why give the third one supremacy over the other two?" I had to wonder.

Then it hit me! Here is a multi-layered, triple-faceted declaration about God's intervention in time and space. Paul describes a place where past, present, and future meet. A holy intersection governed by the great *"I Am."* This is the same *"I Am"* that appeared to Moses in the burning bush (Exodus 3:14). The "I Am" that the disciples witnessed *"walking on the water"* (John 6:16-21). The "I Am" that *"is the same yesterday and today and forever."* The "I Am" that will reappear on the final day of history as *"the Alpha and the Omega, the First and the Last, the Beginning and the End"* (Revelation 22:13). Just as the prophet Daniel recorded his vision of the distant future, Paul recorded what the Holy Spirit revealed to him about the dimensions of time and space.

Faith, hope, and love are the sacred forces that fill and sustain everything!

What is faith?

Faith has its roots in the sub-dimension of *the past*. As the New Testament epistles (especially The Letter to the Hebrews) describe the nature of faith, they also explain how it is inherited from those who came before us. Faith is the spiritual mortar that binds together all who have ever believed and connects them (us) to God Himself. Faith is composed of the lessons learned down through the ages about truth and trust. As an illustration, consider the simple act of walking into an unfamiliar room and sitting down on a chair. How do we know it is safe to enter the room? Why do we trust the floor and the chair to bear our weight? How can we know that the walls and ceiling won't collapse on us? We can enter that space and sit down on the chair with confidence because of the many buildings and chairs we have occupied in the past. Our experience has taught us to trust.

This same principle applies to virtually everything we do in life, from getting out of bed each morning…to eating a meal…to getting on an airplane…to spending money…to choosing our friends. All these choices, and the actions that follow, are rooted in lessons we have learned in the past. The same is true as we aspire for greater things, like deciding whom to love or whether to place our trust in God. As we contemplate each of these decisions, we rely on previous experiences. As the old saying goes, "Fool me once, shame on you. Fool me twice, shame on *me*." The past is our greatest teacher.

How important is faith in living life to the fullest? You tell me. Imagine trying to make it through life without the secure foundations others have provided for you in the past. Care. Correction. Education. Moral training. Mentoring. These are the essentials for having a successful future. The past is our launch pad. For me it's inconceivable that anyone can live a full and healthy life, or even function, without being launched from a foundation of faith. Faith is our guide and protector. And where faith is absent, fear abounds.

What about hope?

What is hope? And why is it next on Paul's list of foundational virtues? Just as faith has formed and sustained us in the past, hope propels us into the future. Hope is the second sub-dimension of time revealed in 1 Corinthians 13:13. Hope is faith from the past projected into *the future*. Once we understand that faith has carried us this far, we are much more likely to count on hope to carry us the rest of the way.

As Paul puts it in Romans 8:24, *"For in this hope we were saved. But hope that is seen is no hope at all. Who hopes for what they already have?"* Just as our faith has been formed in the days behind us, our hope is strengthened as we exercise that same faith in the days ahead of us. Thus, what is true of faith is also true of hope. The dynamics are the same. They both help us to accept our past and trust in our future. If we don't have either, fear takes control of our lives.

How important is hope? Again, you tell me. Can you imagine taking another breath without some measure of hope? Hope is what readies us for each new moment and equips us to handle each new day. Without hope, life holds no promise and has no meaning.

That leaves us with LOVE, the third and greatest of life's essential truths.

What is love? How does love complement faith and hope? If faith represents the past, and hope represents the future, where does love fit into this triad? And why is it the finest of the three?

As you may have guessed, love is the divine manifestation of truth in the sub-dimension of *the present*. Love is the power that lifts and sustains us at the sacred place where past and future merge. The past is behind us and cannot be changed. The future is inaccessible and yet to unfold. This leaves the present as the only temporal space we can occupy. The present is dynamic and never static, a string of fleeting moments that we experience but cannot capture. And love is the supernatural resource that God has made available to us as we pass through every precious moment. Love is God's presence within us in the here and now.

The purpose of love is revealed at the moment it appears. Think of it this way. Imagine me saying to you, "You know, I used to love you." I doubt that you would take this as a shower of affection. It's more likely you would be confused. An admission of past love means little or nothing within the context of the present because love is something we crave *right now*. Hearing we have been loved in the past is perplexing, even hurtful. If love is a currency that is valid only in the present—which I believe it is—expressions of past love are meaningless.

In the same way, if I were to say to you, "I sincerely intend on loving you sometime *in the future*," I don't think that would feel like a warm fuzzy. Once again you might ask, "What about today? How do you feel about me *right now*?" While we promise future love in our wedding vows, that promise sounds hollow unless our betrothed has experienced our love in the past. Past performance makes present promises reliable. I can repeat pledges of future love until I'm blue in the face, but it's not until those pledges withstand the test of time that they have any credibility. The validity of any promise in the present will be revealed as it is fulfilled in the future. I repeat, love is a currency valid *only* in the present. And that is by God's design.

It is worth noting that Paul isn't the only one who places love at the top of the list of Godlike virtues. Jesus proclaimed the excellence of love and exhibited such love in his words and actions. Jesus has been called "love with skin on," which is an affirmation of God's unique incarnation in Christ. The Apostle John describes Jesus as the incarnation of divine love in 1 John 4:7-10: *"Dear friends, let us love one another, for love comes from God. Everyone who loves has been born of God and knows God. Whoever does not love does not know God, because God is love. This is how God showed his love among us: He sent his one and only Son into the world that we might live through him. This is love: not that we loved God, but that he loved us and sent his Son as an atoning sacrifice for our sins."*

As we strive to find meaning and fulfillment in every passing moment and with every breath, we should remember that God's presence fills every dimension and sub-dimension of His creation: the cosmic dimensions, the dimension of time, and even the mysterious and yet-to-be-revealed dimensions that God may make accessible to human souls in the metaphysical realm. The reality of God—past, present, and future—is revealed to us and ignited within us as we receive the three highest and finest gifts God has bestowed upon humanity: Faith...Hope...and Love.

And the greatest of these is **LOVE**.

Our emotions will continue to ebb and flow throughout this incredible journey of life. They are an integral part of our existence. As long as we live in this fallen, imperfect world—and until the Lord returns to make right what we have made wrong—we will face the unavoidable troubles of life and the emotions that come with them. This is why we must not allow our vacillating thoughts and fickle emotions to control us. Emotions are like the weather, ever changing from bright to dark, calm to violent, clear to cloudy. They come, and they go. All we can do is learn to control what we do with each thought and emotion.

God runs the outer universe without our input, but He gives us a say in the running of our inner universe. He doesn't intend for us to merely survive, but to *thrive*. And He has provided us with a foundation that will bear our weight in even the worst emotional storm. It is the rock of Jesus Christ. That rock is composed of three essential elements that sustain us in this life and will carry us into the next: Faith, Hope, and Love.

And, again I say, the greatest of these is **LOVE**.

In knowing that **LOVE** is God's greatest gift, and by accepting that gift and letting it flow through us, we are assured that the best is yet to come!

One of the teachers of the law came and heard them debating. Noticing that Jesus had given them a good answer, he asked him, "Of all the commandments, which is the most important?"

"The most important one," answered Jesus, "is this: 'Hear, O Israel: The Lord our God, the Lord is one. Love the Lord your God with all your heart and with all your soul and with all your mind and with all your strength.' The second is this: 'Love your neighbor as yourself.' There is no commandment greater than these."

"Well said, teacher," the man replied. "You are right in saying that God is one and there is no other but him. To love him with all your heart, with all your understanding and with all your strength, and to love your neighbor as yourself is more important than all burnt offerings and sacrifices."

When Jesus saw that he had answered wisely, he said to him, "You are not far from the kingdom of God." And from then on no one dared ask him any more questions. — **Mark 12:28-34**

ACKNOWLEDGEMENTS AND WORDS OF GRATITUDE

I am grateful beyond measure for the following people and their generous support, able assistance, and bountiful encouragement in helping me bring this book to completion:

• My wife Susan: ever faithful, boundlessly supportive, a paragon of patience and understanding. Even though she makes no claim to be a writer herself, she is an avid reader, keen thinker, and much cherished resource. Our conversations—plus her proofreading and suggestions—have contributed greatly to this book.

• The faculty and students of Westminster College at the University of Cambridge in the United Kingdom. Two of my books were written during sabbatical terms at the college. I thank these friends and colleagues for their hospitality and the scintillating discussions over meals and in the local pub. The world's premier institution of higher learning certainly raised the bar and provided inspiration for this author.

• My former employer, Young Life International, and my teammates in student ministry in the Mid-Europe Region. This wild gang has been a source of unfailing support, motivation, and just plain fun. There are no finer companions than those who stand beside us in the trenches on the front line of ministry.

• My longtime friend Tom Hayes and his creative team at Riley Hayes Advertising Agency in Minneapolis for guiding me along and designing the book cover.

• The members of our weekly home group in Lugano, Switzerland who studied and discussed a chapter every week for six months and helped me fine-tune the material, especially Daniel Barrow; Emily Lingeri; Amy and Zach Mulert; Michel Rapelli; Roger and Jane Reissner; Christof, Milo, and Melody Zanecchia; and my life-mate Susan.

• My team of editors. How blessed I am to have such bright, competent, and caring critics to sharpen my thinking and polish my grammar and punctuation! A big thank you to my lead editor, Shubha Paton—she with such a keen eye. And to the following team of readers: Nancy Adams, Candie Blankman, Bruno Boldrini, Douglas Brouwer, Mike Brunner, Doug Fondell, Mike Griggs, Jane and Martin Hasik, Ali Kennedy, Pam and Jürg Kessler, Kathy Michael, Jane Peterson, Dan Remus, Randy Rowland, Marco Schnitter, Jeffrey Schultz, Kit Troedson, John Vawter, Rick Whitehill, John Wilson, Randall Zindler, and Sophie Zweifel.

www.ingramcontent.com/pod-product-compliance
Lightning Source LLC
LaVergne TN
LVHW051503080426
835509LV00017B/1897